I HATE
THE DALLAS COWBOYS

By Thomas R. Pryor

River to River: New York Scenes from a Bicycle
YBK Publishers

I Hate the Dallas Cowboys

tales of a scrappy New York boyhood

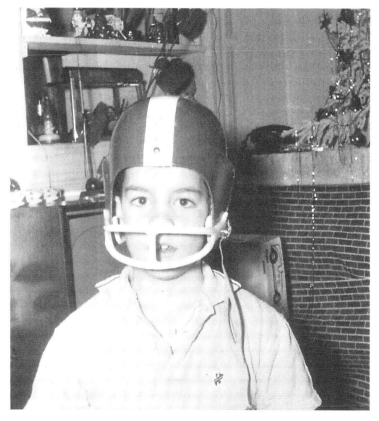

Thomas R. Pryor

YBK Publishers
New York

This book is dedicated to my family,
here and gone,
and principally to my mother,
Patricia Pryor, for her faith in me.

ISBN: 978-1-936411-35-1

YBK Publishers, Inc.
39 Crosby Street
New York, NY 10013
www.ybkpublishers.com

Cover design: Amanda Thorpe

CIP data to come requested 6/18/14

Manufactured in the United States of America for distribution in
North and South America or in the United Kingdom or Australia
when distributed elsewhere.

For more information, visit
www.ybkpublishers.com

60-41

Acknowledgements

Thank you, Robert Marantz, for your care and guidance. Thank you, Barbara Turner, for hearing something in the middle of my babble on our first day at Edenvale, and for nurturing and teaching me and giving me the courage to dive in. Thomas Beller and Patrick Gallagher, thank you for first publishing me and providing a home for my stories.

Thank you, family and friends, for your love and support: Jonathan Calvert, Michele Carlo, Peter Flynn, John Harvey, Jack Hoehlein, The Losers Lounge gang, Kennedy Moore, Eddie O'Donnell, Anne Pechstein, Alison Pryor, Michele Pryor, Edward Rogers, Kristine Simmons, Barry Stabile, Stephanie Uddo, and Eric Vetter.

To my writing family, it would not have happened without you. Thank you, particularly, Zack Hample, Naturi Thomas, Lia Norton, Nicole Ferarro, Merrill Black, Allen Houston, Stefanie Demas, Joyce Greenfield, Ellen Schecter, Dan Rous, Hildy Meltzer, Diana Kash, Susan Shapiro, and Charles Salzberg.

Cris Beam, a thousand hugs for the clarity of your editing, our friendship and your key question, "Tommy, you have a lot of stories. When are you doing a book?" Thank you, John Oudens, for shaping my stories down to their essentials.

Adam Wade, Leslie Goshko, Tim O'Mara, Barbara Aliprantis, Angelo Verga and Robin Hirsch, you're all good eggs. Thank you for teaching me how to turn my stories into verbal movies. Thank you, Amanda Thorpe, for your warm support, our friendship, and your terrific work on the book cover and back cover art. Jaime Nelson and Gordon Balkcom, thank you for your promotional assistance.

Thank you, YBK Publishers, for choosing the book and for your patient and professional support. Otto Barz, thank you for your passionate engagement throughout the process. I am grateful for our friendship. Shep would approve.

Francis Flaherty, my exceptional editor and friend, your trust in my writing changed my life. I am indebted to you, Frank, for your stellar editing on the book. You did an amazing job. We sat on the stoop together for a year. It was all good. "It's going to be a great summer."

About the Author

Thomas R. Pryor is a writer, storyteller and photographer living in New York City. His work can be found on his blog: "Yorkville: Stoops to Nuts."

Contents

Street Kid   1962–1967

Cowboys to Girls   1967–1972

xiv   I Hate the Dallas Cowboys

"Delivery!" shouts the store manager and I barely beat out another stock boy for the job. I've earned the right to visit Mrs. Purtz, a frazzled, beautiful mother of four whose housedress has faulty buttons.

Demon Dachshund   265
My girlfriend's dog was bred to hunt badgers and other hole-dwelling animals. There are no hole-dwelling animals on 83rd Street. But there is me.

The Growler   268
Nan's pride is her windowsill flower boxes. But how she chooses to fertilize them reveals a different emotion altogether.

Back In the Bullpen   274
I become founder and president of the Sparky Lyle Fan Club, and Sparky finds a way to thank me.

Introduction

This book was born in the early 1960s, on my family's roof in Yorkville on Manhattan's Upper East Side. Back then, on hot summer nights after dinner, Dad would grab every extension cord in our apartment, dash to the roof two floors above, pass the cords down to me as I leaned out the backyard window, and then come down to plug it all in. My brother Rory and I would gather chairs, comics, and drawing materials. Dad would lug up our portable TV, beer, iced tea, a spaghetti pot filled with ice, our two Flintstone drinking glasses, and Mom's favorite standing lamp.

Once settled on the roof, we'd watch the fading sunlight slip down the bricks on the tall buildings on East End Avenue. Soon, dusk would become dark and the only light would come from the lamp next to my father, who would draw. Talking with Dad in the shadows of the neighborhood, surrounded by the silhouettes of water towers, I felt the past transform into a film. I asked about everything: his youth, my grandparents' youths, his friends, Yorkville. His long, detailed answers were saturated with colorful stories.

Rory on the roof, catching up on his reading.

Many other members of my family were splendid tellers of tales, too, especially Dad's mother, Nan Rode, who lived around the corner. At 5 years old, I'd run around the block to her building, rush up the stairs and into her living room, and then drag her red leather hassock into the kitchen. I'd take off the top and there, nestled inside, were all of Nan's family photos. She was always exasperated with me because I liked to yap while Nan liked to get the show on the road. But I'd force her to tell me everything she knew about every photo, from the earliest one—a 1906 shot of her mother pregnant with Nan, at the family fruit stand on 75th Street and Avenue A—right down to the latest picture. Merging my family's photographs with their stories built a cinematic record of the neighborhood in my mind with clear voices, characters, and places.

I also learned to love storytelling from Jean Shepherd. I'd listen to his conspiratorial delivery on late night radio—we were in cahoots!—and he would take me on wild journeys that I could never imagine would end safely but always did. I spent countless hours listening to outlandish tales from TV's Sandy Becker and Chuck McCann, too. McCann was out of his mind, and his show harmonized beautifully with Becker's wild characters, songs, puppets, trivia, and cartoons.

I cherished Shepherd, Becker, and McCann even more because their eccentricities mirrored those of my own loving but screwball clan:

There was Dad, a terrific artist, amateur photographer, and charmer with a temper and touchiness that made him able to see someone give him the finger through a wall. His anger and talent stewed together in the same pot, and it was hard to tell which would be served next. Mom, nicknamed "Uncle Mommy," would hamstring Dad any chance she could, and he deserved it. You'll read about Mom's dark side in "Murder by Dusting," but you'll also see her unconditionally crazy love throughout the book.

Of course, I have conventional sweet family memories. My Mom's mother, Helen Ryan, would serve me tea with

Carnation evaporated milk; her father, Lennie, was the best hand-holder of all my adult minders and he loved the job. But the bizarre outscored the normal in my family. Pop Ryan set up impenetrable border crossings in his apartment between those rooms that had air-conditioning and those that didn't; once you were in the Arctic Zone, you could not emigrate for any reason. Dad's stepfather, Pop Rode, had a three-part musical snore, and Rory and I would compose songs around it, aided by a toy piano. As for Rory himself, he wandered off so relentlessly as a toddler that my Aunt Barbara and Aunt Joan once tied him to a picnic bench at Orchard Beach.

I am a lucky storyteller because wacky families make for good tales. But the stories are not just about my family. They're also about Yorkville, in part because my family has broad roots in the neighborhood. My two sets of grandparents lived in railroad flats, one half a block away from us and the other two blocks away (we called both couples Nan and Pop). My godmother, Joan, was three blocks away. With this close-knit geography, Rory and I would travel from family house to family house, taking advantage of our kinfolk's open door policy.

Our local origins were deep. Mom's family called East Harlem home starting in the 1880s; they moved to Yorkville in 1942. Nan Rode's family has been in Yorkville since 1896; her brother played alongside actor Jimmy Cagney on the Yorkville Nut Club, a successful turn-of-the-century sandlot baseball team. Nan was a Democratic district leader, and no fewer than three mayors and one governor—Wagner, Koch, Dinkins and Mario Cuomo—called her "The First Lady of Yorkville." She knew everyone in the district and that meant that as a kid I was doomed to be good. Everything I did got back to her.

My stories are also about street life because, in the 1960s and 1970s, and unlike today, childhood happened as much outside as it did in your home. A host of colorful characters loomed large in local kids' lives back then. To name a few, there was Herman the German, the barber who gave us our dreaded crew cuts; the grumpy Mr. Moylan, who never threw our Spaldeens back when they sailed through his open window; and Joe, the sole employee of Spotless Cleaners, who was my biggest "catch" mentor besides Dad.

My Hat Trick

What was this working-class urban neighborhood like for a kid? It was TV's *The Wonder Years*, except we had subways. Here's a scene to give you a sense of that time in that place.

A dime was the going-rate donation a kid in the 1960s could expect, but I typically reached for the stars and asked my adult relatives for a quarter. It was the running joke in all the households. But once in a blue moon I'd get three of them to say, "Yes," and when they did I had movie money—75 cents for the Loews or the RKO. Then I would go see a new film by my lonesome, running all the way up 86th Street where the theaters were.

The heart of Yorkville thumped away under 86th Street, between First and Lexington Avenues. Between those points or right off them were the pleasure domes of my childhood. The movie houses, Cushman's Bakery, the Heidelberg Restaurant, Berlin Bar, Merit Farm, Papaya King, Ideal Restaurant, and the butcher shops, Karl Ehmer and Schaller & Weber. Prexy's offered "The Hamburger With a College Education" and Salamander Shoe Store lured kids in with a free air-filled balloon on a straightened metal hanger (they were too cheap to buy helium). I learned to gamble at Woolworth's, where you could win a jumbo banana split for just a penny, and I ate countless crocks of mac and cheese at Horn & Hardart, the legendary automat.

My family has played, shopped, fought and gallivanted along 86th Street for the past hundred years.

The *WPA Guide to New York City*, first published in 1939 and reprinted in 1992, says Yorkville runs from 59th Street north to 96th Street, and from the East River west to Lexington Avenue. This does not coincide with my three generations of knowledge of the neighborhood. My family would swear that Yorkville's southern border was in the low 70s and that its western edge included Central Park. Rich people may have lived in the fancy houses west of Lexington Avenue, but Central Park was ours.

The *Guide* continues: "Popularly synonymous with the German quarter, Yorkville in reality is a much more inclusive section." True. There were the Irish, such as my boyhood friends Paddy McNamara and Steve Murphy, and Hungarians, like my classmate Attila Krupincza, and Jews, and Italians, and more. Yorkville was very inclusive. The characters in my yarns range from my teachers, the Sisters of Divine Charity, to Freddie Hammer, the neighborhood junkie. The mothers mostly stayed at home; the fathers worked as cops, sanitation men and salesmen (my dad sold freight space for the Barber Lines shipping company).

I grew up in the New York City of open hydrants, nickel Devil Dogs, stickball and nuns who slugged you for humming baseball beer jingles in class. My father took me to saloons and we stayed all day, and no one thought it was strange. My mother called the stroller "the family car." We didn't have a real one.

This book is essentially true, both in the events and people it describes, with these exceptions: A very few names, dates and locations were changed to protect privacy, and to give narrative shape; a few details are altered, a few characters and events are composites, and some timelines were expanded or compressed. Some dialogue is reconstructed. Of course, I have been faithful to my memory, but memory can play tricks. Still, this collection of stories describes the emotional truth of my experience of growing up absurd in Yorkville.

The book has 53 linked stories and related photographs. A sample photo album: a shot of my mother with her finger up her nose, giving my father the business for annoying her peace; a 1935 snapshot of my grandfather's hack license; and sweet pictures of Rory and me swimming in Central Park's

Bethesda Fountain. In other words, family life with an urban edge.

Mostly, these tales are about my youth, my first 18 years, and so it is about everything that kids are—rambunctious, goofy, sensitive, dumb—and it dwells on their big themes: parents and school, sports and romance, food and music. Here are a few trailers from the home movies that will follow:

- In a standoff with a nun who demanded I finish my lunch, I sculpt the detested white beans on my plate into a crucifix. It was my bid for mercy.
- At Yankee Stadium in 1961, a friend of my dad, a former minor league ballplayer, hoists me over the bullpen fence to greet the star reliever, Luis Arroyo. I am agog. I'm on sacred ground. In 1972, I return to the Yankee bullpen.
- In retaliation for her sons' piggish ways, Mom executes Jerry Mahoney, our beloved dummy. She then becomes a sneaky serial killer of many other toys in a quest for order and space.
- In a friend's basement, my buddies and I furnish a teenage make-out lair we called the Leopard Lounge. The centerpiece: a castoff couch we had whisked from curbside just as the garbage truck was bearing down.

You probably get the picture, but come sit on the stoop with me for just one more. It's early June 1964. There's a manhole cover in the middle of the street and it is about to explode and soar three stories into the air. Down below, lovingly parked and polished, is Pete Palermo's cherished Thunderbird convertible, with its candy-striped seats and its vulnerable canvas top. The manhole cover starts to descend. . .

The Early Years
1952–1964

Fort Sumter

Being with my parents means entering a war zone.
One memorable clash: The Battle of the Broken TV.

During the first year of my parents' marriage, 1952, my mother was shot dead. Anticipating her bridegroom's imminent arrival home from work, Mom smeared her flowery housedress with ketchup and lay down on the shiny linoleum floor. To add realism, she took the pointy gold tip of a small American flagpole, rubbed her makeshift bullet in ketchup and placed it carefully beside her prone body. Giving short shrift to my father's easy-to-frighten factor, there on the cold clean floor she died as Dad climbed the four flights to their honeymoon castle.

Temporarily unable to find an apartment in Yorkville, their neighborhood on Manhattan's Upper East Side, my parents had taken over a cousin's place in Woodside, Queens. In the living room of the sunny pre-war space, Artie Shaw's sweet clarinet lifted from the record player as it played "Begin the Beguine," floating tender music in the air.

There are two versions of what happened when Dad opened the door.

"Your father screamed like a girl and fell to his knees," said Mom. "His tears leaked on my face as he pulled me up for a reenactment of Michelangelo's Pietà. I said 'Boo!' and shot laughing spit across his face. Hearing Dad's keening wails, Peggy Mearns, my best friend in the whole world, ran in from the apartment across the hall. Peggy found us disembraced. I was still giggling on the floor, while your dad worked a sponge over several stains on his suit and mumbled obscenities."

Mom said they didn't talk for four days.

Dad's version: "I walked in and immediately knew your Mom was just fine and being a ninny. She grew furious at

Mom and Dad on their wedding day, 1952.

my indifference. She got up and roughly hugged me, causing the ensuing suit stains. Peggy Mearns did come into
the apartment, but rather than join your mother's celebra-
tion, she sadly shook her cute Irish head side to side in a
steady rhythm and said slowly, 'Poor Patty, you need help.
You really need professional help.' "

Dad also said they didn't talk for four days. That is
the story's single matching fact if you don't count Peggy's
appearance. This was the overture to my parents' 46-year
opera.

Mom's aim was true. Her bullshit-gun targeted Dad and
rarely missed. If he started in on her or began delivering his unique gospel from the Book of Bob, Mom would

pick up an imaginary phone and answer, "Ha-no, ha-no." Dad had a speech impediment, and despite all his efforts, he couldn't get L's into his "Hello." No matter how hard he tried, once the phone rang and he answered it, he was trapped into saying, "Ha-no." My younger brother Rory and I found this remarkable on two levels: One, why Dad never thought to change his telephone greeting to "Good morning" or, when he was at work, "Barber Shipping Lines." Two, why Dad never learned to hide this massive red button from Mom. Every time Mom answered her imaginary phone, I'd watch Dad's head turn into a teapot as I shifted uneasily from foot to foot, waiting for the steam to shoot out of his ears.

Being with my parents meant entering a war zone. The space was negotiated rather than shared. My brother Rory and I played an assortment of survival games. One essential game was "Mum." We'd try to see who could go the longest without saying a word. Whoever lost got a punch in the arm. Dad invented "Mum" as an antidote for his frequent hangovers. He liked it quiet when he wasn't speaking. His hangover cocktail of choice—TV and a long game of "Mum."

Once, in 1960, it was the TV that was caught in one of my parents' many crossfires.

It wasn't working and Game Seven of the Yankees–Pirates World Series was less than two hours away. Dad had pulled the set away from the wall and had taken the rear panel off with a screwdriver.

"You know nothing about TVs," my mother said. "Call Dominick."

"It's a loose wire or a blown tube, I know it."

"Thick as a brick..." Mom said, and left the room. Dad stuck his tongue out. I was betting on Dad in this match. Whatever broke, he fixed it...my toys, bike, everything.

While Dad operated on the TV, I paced back and forth with my hands behind my back so I didn't whack anything. I was nervous about whether he would fix the TV in time.

It was a school day, but Dad had let me play half a day of hooky from first grade so I could watch the game.

Dad and I watched all the games together. Dad got excited when the Yankees won. He did the same thing when the football Giants won. I wanted to bottle that excitement and keep it around for the bad days. I learned to root when he rooted. I learned how and when to yell at the TV when the teams played poorly.

Concentrating on my hands, I nearly took a header when I walked into his toolbox. I danced myself back up.

"Tommy, go sit down."

"Can't I help?"

"No, when I'm done, you can help me push it back and plug it in."

"OK," I said, kicking one of my feet into the other.

Finally, Dad said, "That should do it."

I began to help. I knew that he had told me I could help him with two things. I didn't remember which thing came first. When I thought Dad was done, even though his head was still inside the TV, I stuck the plug back into the wall socket.

Dad lit up. The Christmas tree lighting ceremony at Rockefeller Center came to mind.

"I killed him," I whispered. I had heard the story of Mom staging her death for Dad before I was born, but this wasn't an act.

I stared down at my father. His eyes were glazed over, but open. This was good, because I didn't think you could be dead with your eyes open. My brain switched positions.

"If he's not dead, he's going to kill me."

Looking him over, I saw he was dribbling and his belly was moving swiftly in and out. My heart was racing in time with his belly. I touched my chest.

"I'm so dead."

Rory popped his head into the doorway. His eyes were wide open like Eddie Cantor singing "Making Whoopee." Once Rory saw that Dad was alive, and that I was probably going to get into trouble, he signaled Mom by starting to cry. Only then did my mother come into the room from the kitchen. She lifted Rory out of the way and looked down at Dad.

"I told you to call Dominick," she said with a headshake.

After Dad pulled himself together, we called Dominick. Mom grinned and Dad fumed. After a long game of Mum, Dad said, "Tommy, let's go downstairs and wait for Dominick on the stoop."

On the stoop, we didn't talk. Dad was sore at me, but not in the mood to yell or lecture. He didn't look well. His hair stuck straight up in places it was usually lying down. I stared at the top of his head for a long time looking for a sign of smoke. My nerves were shot. When I'm nervous I do lots of talking. Each time I felt my mouth start to open, I'd put both my hands over it. As my worry grew, I began to eat my fist. Dad looked at me like I was nuts, but I just kept chewing away on my hand.

"What the hell are you doing?" he said.

I tried to answer through my fingers. "Nothing, everything's fine."

"I can't understand a word. Get your hand out of your mouth and tell me what you're saying."

Freed to talk, I let 'er go.

"I want the Yankees to win by 15 runs. I want Mickey Mantle to hit four homers. I want a Yankee parade. I want Dominick."

I slumped against Dad's side. He put his arm around me. I pressed my head against his chest to hear his heart. He squeezed me twice. I squeezed him twice.

"Dad, I'm sorry I almost killed you."

He started to laugh. He pulled my head up to see my eyes. He stopped laughing when he saw I was crying. His look changed. His face was so full of love it scared me. He started to cry a little and put my head back on his chest. He kissed the top of my head. I liked when he kissed me. After a couple of minutes, we started to talk. He asked me whether I had learned a lesson.

"Yes, always push the TV back to its right spot before I plug it back in."

He laughed and said, "Yeah, something like that."

We got itchy waiting for Dominick. Our heads craned over the stoop railing to see all the way up the street. Dad stood to stretch. I stretched, too. I saw Dominick's swinging right arm before I saw the rest of him. He rounded the corner with his magic bag—the black leather one with the secret parts to make our sick TV well.

Mom met the three of us at the apartment door. Rory was standing between her legs peeking out from under her housedress. He looked like a little Samson ready to knock Mom's legs down and collapse the temple.

Mom spoke to Dominick while looking directly at Dad. "Dominick, it's so good to see you. Your ears must be burning. Bob and I were talking about you earlier today."

My father's lips moved noiselessly. I was a certified Mom and Dad lip reader.

"I will get you," he said.

Dominick knelt behind the TV. Mom stayed in the kitchen with Rory. Dad and I stood behind Dominick. Dave Seville and the Chipmunks were on the radio singing "I Told the Witch Doctor."

It was 40 minutes to game time. Dad studied Dominick carefully for two reasons. One, to avoid further eye contact with Mom; and two, to collect important information so he could make the repair next time.

Dominick finished in 20 minutes. We'd see the pregame show!

After Dominick drank some iced tea, I carried his bag to the front door with two hands. I stood at the top of the hallway stairs, watching him go down and around each flight, saying good-bye and thank you to the top of his head several times. I stayed there until I heard his last "So long" fade as the lobby door shut behind him.

I ran back into the living room as the Gillette razor commercial music signaled the start of the World Series broadcast.

I dove onto the couch, swinging my legs over Dad's lap. Looking back over my shoulder, I spied Mom's head in the kitchen doorway. She made a funny face and wiggled her nose. I made a face, acknowledging she had won the battle.

Rory

*Dad hates the name Rory. So Mom
manages to give the name to both of their sons.*

The apartment in Woodside overlooked the No. 7 El train and the Long Island Rail Road. The two lines crisscrossed; one train rattled over the other train all day long. It was March 1954, a year after Mom's ketchup-smeared death on the kitchen floor.

"I need food!" Patty pleaded, rubbing her big belly in the kitchen.

"There's plenty of food," Bob answered, playing with the bunny ears on top of the living room TV.

"YOU'RE A LIAR!" Patty opened the refrigerator and eyed the contents for the fifth time in five minutes.

"There's no food-food, only junk. I want bread, I want bacon, I want Hellman's mayonnaise!"

Disregarding her request, Bob shook ice into the spaghetti pot that was chilling his six bottles of Rheingold. Wiping his hands on a dish towel, he definitely heard Patty's next statement: "Get off your bony ass and get me food!"

Bob ignored this, too. It was "Friday Night at the Fights" and he'd just settled in—first round, first beer. Desiring perfect comfort, Bob moved a hassock over to put his feet up. While doing this, he missed the left hook that sent one of the boxers to the canvas with a thud. Unfortunately, Bob's man was down. So was Bob, $20. After the stiff was counted out, the telecast went to a commercial. Disappointed, but now available for chores, Bob wrapped his arm around his extremely pregnant wife's head.

She pushed him away. "Get off. You know I hate anyone touching my head."

Bob bent over, kissed Patty's cheek and asked her softly, "What do you need, Hon?"

Patty reeled off five items, and aimed her lips up to kiss Bob on the mouth.

Back from the store, Bob put his beers in the fridge, washed the pot, and put water on for spaghetti. Grabbing a black frying pan, he made two bacon sandwiches with extra mayo on Silvercup bread. After serving Patty both sandwiches, he took a beer and joined her at the kitchen table.

"So, we're decided on baby names, right?" Bob said. "Marc Anthony if he's a boy, and Alison Leigh if she's a girl."

Bob smiled. Patty did not.

"You're so full of shit. The girl's name is fine. When you name the boy Marc Anthony, be sure you walk carefully over my dead body. Because that's the only way that stupid guinea name will ever appear on my son's birth certificate."

Bob's expression fell.

"Oh, cut the crap and get that stupid puss off your face."

"So what name do you want?"

"Rory," she said.

"Huh?"

"R-O-R-Y, Rory."

"Like Calhoun, the movie cowboy?"

"Yes, it's an old Gaelic name meaning Red King."

"Red? Our hair is black. It's a girly name—you're guaranteeing he'll get the shit kicked out of him."

It grew quiet. The only sound in the room was Patty's low hum. She loved bacon.

Fracturing the silence, Bob said, "It'll be Rory when Brooklyn wins the World Series."

"I'll alert the press."

Bob said, "Give me an alternative."

"Nope," Patty said in between bites.

"Then I'll give you one: Thomas."

"That's inspired." Patty pointed her sandwich at Bob. "I thought we agreed, no fathers' names?"

"It's my brother's name, too."

"You mean we're going to name him after Stone Face?"

"That's my compromise. You'll get to name the next baby."

Patty swallowed a large bite of mayo, with a little bit of bacon and bread attached to it. She chewed slowly, wiped her mouth, and said, "OK."

On March 20th, Patty gave birth to an eight-pound boy. When the nurse let Bob into the recovery room and he saw Patty cradling the baby, he started to cry.

"Oh stop your blubbering and give me a kiss."

"How do you feel?"

"Not too swift," Patty said, wiping sweat from her brow.

Bob, lightly rubbing the baby's dark hair, asked, "How's Tommy?"

"Doctor said he's fine. Isn't he beautiful?"

Bob picked up the wrinkled, red-faced boy. He thought the baby's head looked like a grapefruit. A gorgeous grapefruit. Bob held the baby for a long time, then returned him to Patty.

"I have to fill out the birth certificate. I was thinking about Robert as a middle name," Bob said.

"No," she answered.

"Why not?"

"You picked the first name. I pick the middle name."

"No, no, no, you get to name the next baby."

"No, I get to name the next baby's first name, and you get to name the next baby's second name."

"But…" Bob said, uselessly.

"No buts." Patty closed the discussion. "Tommy's middle name is Rory."

That night, Bob temporarily parked his anger over Mom's choice of middle name, and hailed a cab to his old Manhattan neighborhood. He celebrated his first son by dancing on the bar in Loftus Tavern on 85th Street and York Avenue. A month later, the boy was christened, Thomas Rory. When the priest repeated the boy's second name, Bob rolled his eyes.

A year and a half later, Thanksgiving 1955, Bob and Patty told their families they were expecting again. Throughout the pregnancy, Patty kept Bob in the dark about names. He

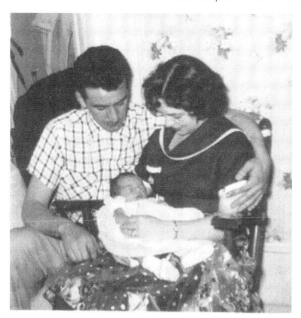

Dad and Mom doting on newborn me.

begged and whined for hints. Late in Patty's term, Bob tried to bribe her by hiding candy bars around the apartment, promising to reveal locations only if she told him the name. Patty never cracked.

On June 20th, 1956, Patty gave birth to a perfect boy. Bob dropped Tommy off with Bob's mother and went directly to the hospital. The room was dimly lit; the baby was sleeping in Patty's arms. She gave Bob a weak wave. He went over to kiss mother and son. Patty gently held Bob's arm, keeping him close. She tilted her head, signaling him to lean in so she could whisper something. Bob pressed his ear to Patty's dry lips.

"Rory, his name is Rory," she said.

Bob backed away. "That's nuts—we've already got a Rory."

"Shush! Middle names don't count. You promised."

Bob knew he'd been had. In desperation, he blurted, "His middle name is Robert."

"Who cares?" she said.

Patty settled back into bed, gave Bob a sly smile and squeezed her Rory tight.

The Family Car

We're city kids, and so the stroller is our Chevy.
But we don't need a motor to get into trouble.

"Get off and start walking," Mom said. Her leg poked my leg, the one twisted over the stroller's front safety bar. "You're six years old."

"No, I'm tired," I said.

My brother bit my hand and I screeched. Only four years old, Rory had sharp, strong teeth. He chewed on anything and gleefully chomped away while trying to bend my fingers backward off the stroller's rail.

"Tommy, for the last time, walk."

"No."

"Please stop. It's so friggin' hot."

"Can't."

"You're too old."

"Not true."

Mom's arm swung over my ducking head.

"Do you want to die?"

"Yes."

"I'll do it. I'm going to make you die, and then you're gonna be dead."

She swept her leg at me judo-style, trying to knock me off. People passing by had their mouths wide open and spun around to stay with us. You usually have to pay for this kind of entertainment.

"Tommy, you're going to fall off and go under the wheels."

"Good, just like the chariots in *Ben-Hur*."

The movie reference disarmed Mom and gave me the opening I needed. Scrambling over my brother's body, I secured myself behind him in the stroller. Mom mumbled curses. I rode for a block before taking my hands off the top of my head, waiting for the smack.

15

With Rory in the "family car" on York Avenue, 1957.

Our stroller was the family car. It was a sturdy kid buggy with a flexible hood that protected everything but the front passenger's feet. There was a running board on each side for vaulting in and out. The tires were white walls. It doubled as a shopping cart, and sometimes Rory and I were forced to walk or be smothered under packages.

On this hot Saturday in August, Mom had us out of the gate early. We had no air-conditioning and she could break a good sweat just by flipping through a calendar to the summer scenes. Dad was still in bed. When we were leaving he yelled from two rooms away, "I'll meet you at Bethesda Fountain in an hour."

Heading west we made one detour, to Parker's Grocery. Mom bought us Sunny Dews, orange drinks in tall wax cartons. She said it might hit 100 degrees and we would need the fluids. We knocked them off while talking to our Dad's mom, Ann Pryor Rode, who had her arms resting on the stone windowsill of her apartment right over the store. In mid-conversation, our grandmother leaned forward and said, "It's gonna be a scorcher." Mom wanted to punch her in the face. Dad and his mother enjoyed the heat and liked to rub it in.

Then Mom pushed us straight up 83rd Street toward the park. I gave her a break and walked up the hill from Second to Park Avenue, but while she was rummaging for something in her handbag I jumped back in. When she saw me she groaned. I felt bad, but I didn't get out.

Guilt eventually got to me when we crossed Fifth Avenue into the shade. I left the stroller and started running ahead. Now Rory wanted to kill me because Mom had him strapped in, and probably would have kept him strapped in for several more years if the authorities would have allowed it. Rory was famous for his chronic running away. Once, at Orchard Beach, Mom's sisters, Barbara and Joan, were forced to tie him to a picnic bench with a bed sheet.

Headed south, we passed the Metropolitan Museum of Art and entered Central Park at 79th Street; it was near the family's favorite sleigh spot, which we called Cherry Hill. When you are six, Cherry Hill makes for a fine mountain as your Dad rides the sled like a cop car chasing a bank robber on a winding road, and you hang on for dear life, the snow flying off the sled's blades, smacking you in the face.

We proceeded to the park's East Drive and walked to the hill at 72nd Street where the majestic Pilgrim statue stands between the trees. In the summer he virtually disappears behind the leaves.

I helped Rory, who'd been sprung from the stroller, to the top of the statue's pedestal and tried to hold his legs. Then he began pointing wildly down the hill.

"Mom, Sailboat Lake, take us around Sailboat Lake!"

He jumped down on my head. We fell, got up, and climbed back into the stroller. Mom clipped the curb when she drove

Bethesda Fountain, our swimming hole.

us off the walkway and up the berm to the top of the hill overlooking the water. After a short pause the carriage started flying down the bumpy knoll. Mom veered the carriage sharply and pushed it slightly out of her reach, yelling, "Runaway babies! Runaway babies! Please, dear God, somebody save my runaway babies!"

Rory and I hung onto each other, one big ball of kid. We used our butts to press against the sides of the stroller, just enough so we still flew freely, but didn't take a header. To help Mom out, Rory and I screamed at the top of our lungs, "Momma, Momma, Momma! Save your precious babies!"

"I'm trying darlings, but this might be our last ride. I don't know if I can hold on much longer. I'm plumb out of strength."

Mom brought us to a screeching halt just before we joined the ducks and sailboats in the pond. With a swipe of her arm across her forehead, she said, "Thank you, Jesus, Mary, and Joseph."

Satisfied with a fine ride and a good job by Mom, Rory and I rode along quietly until we both saw the practically new Alice in Wonderland statue up ahead, the best statue in the world. And nobody was on it! Thrilled, we started to climb and immediately jumped off, yelling "Owwww!" and rubbing our burned hands against our shorts. When it's well over 90 degrees do not climb bronze statues sitting in the sun.

Wet and goofy.

"Dad's meeting us, let's go," Mom said after the pain had subsided. I grabbed Rory's hand and we headed for Bethesda Fountain, and saw Dad sitting on the rim of the fountain pool.

After giving Dad a hug, we begged our parents to let us take a dip in the fountain. Their body language said no, but soon their mouths said, "I don't care," one after the other. We stripped to our briefs and vaulted over the stone wall into the water. The swim lasted a long time. There was a patrolman watching us, but he left us alone. Then his sergeant came by and the patrolman became a cop again. "OK kids, get out of there and stay out," he said with a grin, facing away from his boss.

After our swim Dad said he needed to drop by his mother's; he was concerned she might have blown a fuse in all this heat. Mom didn't care that Dad was running off. She wanted a frankfurter from Papaya King, so the three of us strolled down 86th Street. At Lexington Avenue, my stomach moaned. I saw my favorite food place on earth, Prexy's, with its slogan "The Hamburger with the College Education." Across the street was Nedick's, famous for their hot dogs served on a piece of crappy folded toast that reminded me of my least favorite white bread, Taystee. Nedick's questionable orange drink came in a paper cup stuck in a metal holder. When you ordered a drink the guy behind the counter rapped a holder on the top of a tower of paper cups and when he pulled it off you had a nifty drinking vessel. Not one of my favorites, but Nedick's was there when you were hungry and in a rush to get to the uptown IRT subway. You wolfed down the crappy hot dog on the train. It was and still is a New York tradition to eat on the run.

I figured Papaya King was as close as I would ever get to Hawaii. At the counter, below the counter, and over the counter were all the tropical trappings: coconuts, coconut leaves that looked like hula skirts to me, plastic hula girls, posters of the South Pacific and plastic exotic fruit. Mom, Rory, and I each had a frank and we split one large papaya drink for good luck.

I knew Mom had temporarily lost her mind from the heat when we passed several shoe stores without her even window-shopping. The deadly humidity drove her directly back to our apartment house. I helped her carry the stroller down to the cellar, where we parked our family car for the night.

Blue Feet and Banana Splits

It's dress-up photo day, I'm wearing wool, and I'm not happy. But I learn that if a kid tries hard enough, he can center his legs so they never touch his itchy pants.

The only time I remember Rory and me being squeaky clean for a whole hour was in the fall of 1960, when Mom took us to a photography studio on Third Avenue.

I am repelled by wool. I can't even look at someone wearing it without itching. That morning, Mom made us put on black wool pants and red wool sweater vests. Having a shirt under the vest was useless. In my mind, the wool was right on my skin just as it was on my legs. Mom scrubbed our necks and washed our ears and put Brylcreem in our hair. I hate oil on me, too.

On the way over, Rory was in the stroller and I was about a half block behind them trying to walk in such a way that my legs centered in the pants so no wool would make contact with my skin. Every step was calculated. Because we were late, Mom left Rory unattended a few times to come back to drag me. When she did, Rory unstrapped himself, climbed out, and ran back toward us.

We arrived 25 minutes late. Otto, the photographer, was livid. His bald head was dotted with sweat and he was breathing heavily like Mr. Fields, the landlord in the "Abbott and Costello" TV show. Meanwhile, Rory and I had a fight over who'd ride Otto's hobby horse. It had four springs; so you could go up and down but also get a little side-to-side action. Mom grabbed me off the horse in a headlock. Seeing this, Rory cheered up.

Otto readied his equipment and Mom quickly combed our hair and moved us into position and said, "Smile nice, not stupid, or I'll kill you."

Rory, extremely photogenic, nailed his pose and I didn't screw it up. After Otto snapped the picture, I saw Mom smiling and looking at us like the last hour never happened.

I thought we'd go straight home and I could get out of the monkey suit, but Mom had another plan: we were already on Third Avenue so why not go shoe shopping?

She always complained that her feet hurt. We'd go in and out of shoe stores—Miles, A.S. Beck, and National, to name three—and hunt for that perfect, comfy shoe that she never found. Our routine was predictable. Rory and I would play on the rolling ladders, flying back and forth across the floor, hanging off with one arm free. This usually stopped when either the clerk or Mom threw something at us. Then we'd pick up the foot-measurer. It was metal and its side measuring knobs made it look like it held a secret hidden code.

Momentarily clean and combed, 1960.

In the first store we visited after the photos, Rory tried on spiked heels that he had grabbed from the front window display. He wobbled up and down the carpet, smiling from side to side. I studied him, my hand on my chin and my elbow on my leg, my head unconsciously swaying along with him as he traveled back and forth, back and forth, on his private catwalk.

Rory and I liked two shoe stores best, although we weren't going to them that day. One was Salamander Shoes on 86th Street; the other was Buster Brown's on 83rd. Each store had a kid gimmick. Uncle Norman in Buster Brown's always made sure he knew your birthday. Then he'd send you a birthday card. Six months later, he'd send you another card wishing you a happy half-birthday. I'd get my half-birthday card and say out loud, "Boy, that Uncle Norman is one swell guy. Hey Mom, I need a new pair of shoes. What do you think?"

Mom would deliver a look. First of all, I never cared whether I had any shoes, much less new ones. I cared only about new sneakers. The single thing that triggered my getting a new pair of shoes was a good rainstorm after a hole had developed in my sole. Either I'd get home from school and Mom would notice my socks were wet, or I'd take off my blue school socks and Mom would notice that my feet were blue. Then Mom would say, "Tomorrow we go for new shoes."

The other store's gimmick was a beauty. Salamander was the high-end shoe store in the neighborhood. If you had orthopedic needs, this was the place. That line of products came in handy for me; I often tested the law of gravity by dropping from rarefied heights and my feet took most of the damage. Salamander's ploy was to give you a balloon with every pair of new shoes. What the cheapskates failed to give you was helium. The balloon was nice but filled with boring air. To hold it aloft, Salamander's management attached the balloon to straightened metal shirt hangers. You left the store flying your balloon majestically, but most kids never made it a full block before the metal punctured the balloon, leaving a disappointed kid carrying a straightened hanger with a shred of rubber dangling from its tip.

After giving up on her shoe mission, Mom looked at our sad faces and took us to a coffee shop and ordered three egg creams that we stretched by emptying all the coffee creamers on the diner's counter into our glasses. This drove the waitress crazy and led to our early exit.

Still hungry, we wandered over to Horn & Hardart. Mom, Rory, and I ate crocks of mac and cheese while Mom told us a story about the place.

"It's not like the old days," she began. "When I was a kid you could spend hours in this automat with just a few nickels in your pocket. Steaming coffee came out of the mouth of a brass dolphin. Best baked beans on earth." After a spoonful of mac and cheese, she continued: "My knucklehead cousin John once put a nickel in a machine to get a glass of milk. Then he yelled, 'train wreck,' and showed me his open mouth full of lemon meringue pie. He was so proud of himself that he forgot to stick a glass under the milk spout. Thinking quick, he stuck his hat underneath the spout and collected the milk the hard way."

Rory and I giggled ourselves silly.

We left the automat and went to our favorite store in Yorkville, Woolworth's Five & Ten, on the northeast corner of 86th Street and Third Avenue. Mom could walk the aisles there for hours looking at fabrics, buttons, curtains, knickknacks, dishes, appliances, and housedresses. Children could browse among toys, books, art stuff, and Halloween costumes that were put out two weeks after school kicked in, giving you six weeks to decide who you were going to be that year: Something exciting like the Wolfman, Superman, or Daffy Duck, or old standbys like a hobo, a ghost, or a doctor. Your choices were endless. Discussions among kids blocking the aisle had to be broken up by store clerks.

Arriving at Woolworth's, Mom made a deal with me.

"I'll meet you at the lunch counter in an hour. It's 2:30, be there at 3:30."

"OK," I said and nodded.

I usually had two things on my mind at these times. Number one was in the basement.

Records! Woolworth's basement was a musical heaven where I could go through a large selection of LPs and 45s. I was just starting to read, but that did not stop me from looking over each one like a fossil, scrutinizing the photos, the few words I could understand, the label color and the different logos of the record companies. American Bandstand was my key learning tool for music.

I stood in front of the record bins for so long, sometimes, that I'd have to pee bad but they never, ever, let you use the bathroom in Woolworth's. It was a waste of time to ask, so instead I did the "pee pee dance." I'd bounce up and down as I went from record row to record row, keeping my legs moving. This drove the clerk crazy.

"Stop dancing!"

"I'm not dancing."

"Your legs are going up and down fast, that's dancing."

"I'm looking. The music in my head is moving my feet."

"That's dancing."

"I can't dance, my Dad says I have no rhythm. Look at me."

"If you don't stop you'll have to leave." Then the clerk stormed away.

This time I was OK; my urge to go wasn't dire. So after a thorough review of all the records, I went upstairs to the lunch counter for the second thing I needed to do—sit on one of those cool red swivel seats and do some quality spinning. I had 20 minutes before Mom picked me up.

Standing by the counter and looking over the seat choices, I noticed above me a row of balloons that ran the length of the counter. Each balloon contained a number, from 1 cent to 39 cents, and that number would be what you paid for a Jumbo Banana Split, with 39 cents being the regular full price. Even if I wasn't hungry, I was intrigued by the possibility of getting a huge prize for only a penny if I picked the right balloon. I walked along the row frantically, eyeing each balloon like a new father who couldn't find his baby behind the nursery glass. Which one? Which one?

Feeling the pressure, I pointed to a blue balloon.

"Miss, Miss, please, I want that one."

The waitress popped the balloon with her hairpin and retrieved the piece of paper inside, held it up and said, "38 cents. Hey kid, you won a penny." She handed me the paper. When I saw the "38" I thought about the 15 cents I had in my pocket and started working my brain. I used my fingers to count it off. 23! I was 23 cents short. The woman asked me what type of hot fudge I wanted. "Chocolate."

I pulled myself up to one of the swivel seats, put my folded hands on the counter and started circling my thumbs. My spinning enthusiasm was put on hold.

"Would you like to swing on a star?"

They ran out of hot nuts so she put a cherry on top. I quickly ate the ice cream, hot fudge and whipped cream, leaving the cherry and the banana. When the waitress gave me the check she saw that I'd left the banana and scratched her head and smiled at me like you would smile at an idiot.

I stayed put. Any minute now Mom and Rory would arrive. Sitting still, I worked on a story, but I didn't have one.

"Tommy!"

I turned and they were there.

"Mom, can you lend me 23 cents?"

Her arm came up and I flinched but her arm went the other way through her thick black hair.

"Why do you need money?"

"I, ummm, tried to win you a banana split for a penny."

Her arm came up again, this time I ducked. The arm was pointing to the balloons. "Don't tell me you did this. You don't like bananas. You need help!"

I had learned there was a certain head position I needed to maintain to calm Mom down. That day I learned two new things: Rory liked wearing pumps and I would try to win a one cent jumbo banana split every time I had a chance.

The Cisco Kid

Our old, vibrating washing machine begins its "chug, chug, chug," and I dash into the kitchen and climb aboard. It's time to ride my bucking bronco through the sagebrush.

"Chug, chug, chug" was all I needed to hear. I'd run from any point in the apartment and jump on. Mom's washing machine was my rocking bronco during morning chores. Old and cranky, it burped, coughed, and passed gas, but it still worked. The machine would lift itself from its corner by the kitchen sink and begin its Ouija board dance across the linoleum floor. I never knew where it was headed. Sick of having to plug it back in when it pulled itself out of the wall socket, Mom added a long extension cord. This gave me a passport to ride the open plains from sink to wall, from wall to door, across the kitchen.

Only one rule applied. I couldn't wear my sneakers. On earlier rides, I'd firmly plant my feet on the wallpaper to maximize lift-off. This left permanent marks resistant to all cleaning products. This displeased Mom. Our compromise? I wore socks. So did Mom. We each wore a pair of Dad's thick hunting socks. Me? I used them to effectively push off as the stagecoach perilously neared the wall. I'd redirect my Pony Express steed out of the sagebrush, back onto the dirt road. Mom used her pair to work. She'd skate across the floor in Dad's socks in a fluid polishing motion until she saw her house-proud smile reflected off the burnished linoleum.

The kitchen radio would be our soundtrack. Or, Mom would put Mario Lanza on the record player. We'd sing at the top of our lungs. The music, the bouncing machine, Mom's cleaning cha-cha and me—a chaotic orchestra playing for just the two of us. We would join Mario in one of our favorite songs.

Giddyup! Sitting on my favorite bronco.

Drink, Drink, Drink,
To eyes that are bright as stars when they're shining
*   on me.*
Drink! Drink! Drink!
To lips that are red and sweet as the fruit on the tree!
Here's a hope that those bright eyes will shine.
Lovingly, longingly soon into mine!
May those lips that are red and sweet,
Tonight with joy my own lips meet!
Drink! Drink! Drink!

We knew every word.

Mornings with Mom were best but we had fun in the afternoon, too. Our small apartment had a tiny living room with a tiny couch where I would park myself when

I was home sick. Bored on one of those off days during second grade, I concocted a torture/tickle game to play on Mom.

For torture I moved the art. Dad was an artist; his paintings and sketches lined the living room walls. While Mom was in the kitchen I quietly left the couch and carefully skewed all the picture frames, but only enough for her to just faintly perceive that they were no longer perfectly straight. My skill was knowing when enough was enough. It was also critical that I return to the couch to resume a sickly pose before Mom came back into the room. When she did, I measured my success by counting the number of twitches on her face as she darted her eyes around the room from frame to frame.

This unhinged her, but she refused to acknowledge it. She would only give me a pathetic look that said, "You don't know what this does to me. Do you like to do this to me? Please don't do this to me. Did you do this to me?" When she could no longer bear it she would chase me in a circle through the rooms until I wore her out.

That's when the tickle part happened. Mom was exhausted, while I was on the road to recovery, so we reversed places. Mom took to the couch and I began to go through the drawers in my room looking for something to do. When Mom's fog turned into a full-blown nap, I put a sock snuggly over each of my ears. Then I worked one of Dad's 45 records onto each ear, pulling the sock through the record's center hole, my ear bent inside like a taco. The socks were now floppy puppy ears.

Then I snuck through my parents' bedroom, past the French doors leading into the living room, and worked my way to the back of the couch. On my knees I rounded the couch, slowly coming face to face with sleeping Mom. Starting in a whisper I began building a soft doggy bark, "Woof, woof, woof ..."—not to frighten her, but, ideally, to wake her dreamily. Out of her daze she started laughing low and sweet. I licked her nose. Laughing harder, Mom pulled my head to hers and kissed my hair and nuzzled me good.

If I compare the sweet days and afternoons I spent alone with Mom to a ride on the Central Park carousel, then my interludes with Dad were like a turn on a rickety Coney Island roller coaster, with loose bolts, broken safety belts, and people getting sick in front of and behind us. We loved each other and shared major interests, but approached them from diametrically different points of view that usually led to multi-car collisions.

Dad had an uncanny skill. We'd be having a conversation, and I knew it was a conversation, but, without my knowing when or how, that conversation became an argument. What did I miss? Desperately I'd search for the point where we'd flipped over, but I could rarely find it. That's why, although I'd love to give you an example of these mystifying transformations, I swear I can't. I knew he couldn't help himself, but that knowledge was useless during the wreck.

Dad got social, but not at home. I tried to go to sleep early on nights he was out, to avoid the noise when he came in. I liked the dark because nothing good happened when Dad switched on a light.

One Friday, when I was 7, I didn't make it into bed and fell asleep on the couch. When Dad came in he tickled me awake and insisted on putting me up on his shoulders for a ride into my bedroom. Up I went like a sack of potatoes, barely missing the living room light fixture. Dad was six feet tall. The apartment's ceiling was a little under eight with two doorways between the living room and my bedroom. No room for error. He was my drunken pony and I was his terrified Cisco Kid who had to drop my neck and head down as we passed through the doorways or get clipped and plummet.

Hurtling through the first doorway, we stumbled into the kitchen. "Wheeeeeeeee," Dad sang as my head cracked a paint chip off the ceiling just before his leg rapped the kitchen table. I struggled to stay on. Dad readjusted me. The next part I enjoyed even less. He had to stop before we made our attempt through the second doorway. I didn't like having that stretch of time to think about what lay ahead.

With a jerk, act two commenced with two drunken circlings of the kitchen and several more "Wheeeeeeees." Then Dad began his assault. Going in much too high, he left me with two choices, neither pain free: Do I fall backward as if I were doing a rodeo trick and hope my father hangs onto my legs? Or do I hold on and let my skull hit the plaster? I decided to hold on and ducked my upper body down to Dad's shoulder, held my breath, and closed my eyes. The hair on my head brushed the top of the doorway, but even with my eyes closed I felt us pass from the light of the kitchen into the darkness of the bedroom.

We were through it. Dad's natural athletic ability was still there even when he was three sheets to the wind. He readjusted me one last time before lifting me off his shoulders and putting his elder sack of potatoes to bed with a kiss.

Hold My Hand

His kids don't like him. His mere name makes my father's
face twitch. But Pop Ryan is a fantastic hand-holder.

My grandfather, Lennie Ryan, "Pop" to us, had three children besides Mom, and I never heard one of them say a nice word about him. Hearing his name made my father's face twitch. Even Mom's sweet-natured mother, Helen Ryan ("Nan"), had nothing good to say about the man. None of this mattered to me. Pop was a fantastic hand-holder.

In 1959, I entered kindergarten at P.S.77, up the block from my grandparents' apartment on York Avenue and 86th

Lounging with Pop Ryan in the backyard, 1956.

34

Street. That year he'd meet me in front of the school every day at noon. I'd burst through the door and there he was—hair slicked back, white dress shirt, belted slacks pulled way up. Kissing was not allowed. I was a boy. Holding hands was permitted and encouraged.

If another kid bugged me about it, I'd say, "Pop is extra careful about crossing the street. He likes to get a good grip before we hit the corner. We're practicing." Even if I didn't have that great excuse, I would have happily suffered the teasing to keep holding Pop's hand.

There was a range of differences among my regular hand-holders. Mom was an exasperated hand-holder because my brother and I held advanced degrees in fidgeting. My other three grandparents were better hand-holders than Mom. Decent grip, not too hard on the fingers, and they usually followed the unwritten rules about when to let your hand go. The "let go" rules included best friend sightings and after crossing the last street within a block of your destination.

Then there was Dad's hand-holding. Crossing a street, Dad held our hands only if we were able to wiggle his hand off our necks. Rory didn't give in easily on the hand-holding, so Dad didn't waste any time and went right for our necks when it was the three of us. Approaching a curb, he'd eye our necks the way a cartoon wolf eyes a lamb that turns into a sizzling roast in the wolf's cartoon thought bubble. His meat hooks would grab our necks from behind, forcing our heads toward the asphalt. Although I developed an appreciation for the varied character of the street beds in my neighborhood (since that was all I could see), I worried about whether Dad knew what he was doing. We never discussed how he had learned to cross streets. I still remember my prayer as we stepped off the curb: "I hope no cars are coming. I hope no cars are coming."

This brings me back to Pop's award-winning hand-holding. Out the school door, I'd scramble across the pavement with the other hatchlings. I'd offer Pop my left hand. He was a righty. I'm a lefty. We danced well together. As we walked

silently down the street, the school noise drifted away behind our backs and we'd play a hand-holding game. I'd make
believe I was letting go, and he'd snatch me back at the last
moment. All future "gotcha" games were measured against
this one.

I smelled his cigar on his clothes. I loved him for giving
me his cigar boxes.

He never said more than, "How are you, Tommy?" or "It's
so good to see you." My certain knowledge that he meant
these words every time he said them was locked away in a
box that no one else could ever open. His hand around mine
took my spirit's pulse and temperature. It made my sadness
and loneliness melt away.

At the corner he gave me a dime to buy two copies of *The
Daily News*. His building had a tall front stoop that nearly
met the curb. We'd sit at the top for maximum view. He'd
read his paper and I'd partially read mine. I knew my alpha-
bet and many of the words in the sports section. Side by side
with Pop on the stoop, I learned every nuance of his ritual:
How to watch people walk by, when to look up, and when to
go back to the paper. I learned that there were certain people
you started looking at earlier and stayed with longer—gener-
ally the skirted gender across a pretty wide age group.

If it was hot, we'd take out the two middle pages and put
them under our bottoms to ease the heat from the stone.
When it was too hot, we'd go inside. In the apartment's
front window was my family's first air conditioner. The
apartment ran lengthwise four rooms in a row, a railroad
flat. During the summer, between the rear fourth room (the
kitchen), and the third room (the living room), Pop Ryan
created an elaborate series of hanging plastics and curtains to trap the cool air. I helped him gather the materials
and tools for this job, including hammers, nails, tacks, and
duct tape. Oddly, he kept his tools in a big wooden shoe-
polishing box and his shoe-polishing items—brushes, tins
of polish, buffing rags, etc.—in a cardboard shoebox. I got
a kick out of that.

Once you moved into the Arctic Zone, Pop made regular announcements—"The Northwest Passage is sealed," or "No boats allowed through the canal." We made up other slogans together, but the message was the same: Once you were in the Arctic Zone, you stayed put.

The curtained area was so well shielded that I imagined an Orthodox Jewish wedding had ended up in the apartment one afternoon. The men danced merrily on one side of the curtain, holding hands and circling the beds, while the women chatted in the kitchen. Enchanted with this company, my grandmother mingled with the group, asking if anyone happened to be related to the Rosenblatts from 85th Street?

When I entered the cool side of the curtain, I always went in with provisions. At first, it was comic books and a snack. Then I learned to take in sweaters. Pop would fall asleep in his chair and no one was allowed to touch the AC controls but him. He'd sleep, the room chilled, and I'd form smoke rings with my breath. After a while, I also learned to bring in a couple of Flintstone grape jelly glasses. That's because once inside I couldn't leave the ice station even to take a pee.

In distress, I'd be in the front room, my lower body hidden behind a chair. Eyes alert to the curtain, I'd unzip my fly and fill up the two glasses. I retained a great track record with this trick until one day when, after peeing, I fell asleep on my grandparents' bed.

A little later, in that twilight summer nap place, I was unsure if I was dreaming or if someone was in the bedroom with me.

"Oh, shit!" Nan said immediately after I heard the ding of one glass hitting another glass. Poor Fred Flintstone and Barney Rubble had toppled to the floor, spilling their contents. Nan left the room and came back with a mop.

After she moved the mop around a few times, the nutty aroma of fresh pee rose up to her nose and she went from minor accident to major cleanup mode, saying, "Why on God's earth did you pee in those glasses? Tommy, what is wrong with you?"

"Nothing."

"Peeing into glasses we drink out of isn't nothing. Not even close."

"I had no choice."

"What's the little room next to the kitchen called?"

We were moving into the sea of unanswerable questions. I was looking for a life preserver.

"A bathroom?"

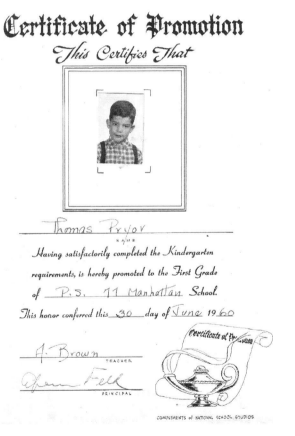

P.S. 77 kindergarten diploma, 1960.

"Right, it's a bathroom and this is a bedroom."

Excuseless, I dropped a dime on Pop.

"Pop won't let me leave."

"What do you mean?"

"He told me to never leave the AC area and go through the curtains unless it was for good."

"Well, leaving for peeing is good."

"No, he meant for good. You know, forever-not-coming-back good. He said that once I was inside the North Pole, I had to hold my pee."

Nan started shaking her head from side to side and left me to go visit Pop napping in the living room. Through the doorway, I saw her bop him on the top of his head. He shot straight up from a deep sleep in his La-Z-Boy lounger.

"You are the cheapest and dumbest Irishman in New York City," she said.

I figured I was going to get it, too, but I didn't. Nan threatened to throw Pop's beloved cigars away if he kept up the asinine Arctic Zone border-crossing rules. And so from that day on, limited bathroom privileges were permitted.

Pop and I continued to hold hands straight through my kindergarten graduation day.

Ladies in Black

I don't really need Sister Beatrice to help me tie my shoes.
But a first grader in love's got to do what he's got to do.

In October 1960, Mom was pulling for Kennedy and Dad was rooting for Nixon. I couldn't have cared less—my thoughts were on baseball. The Pittsburgh Pirates had just crushed my heart by beating the Yankees in Game Seven of the World Series. I wasn't sure if I would ever recover.

The morning after that fateful game, my mother walked me to St. Stephen of Hungary, the Catholic elementary school I attended on 82nd Street. At the entrance I kissed her good-bye and dragged my schoolbag up the four flights of stairs to my classroom. I sat at my desk feeling glum and numb. My melancholy lasted for about an hour until suddenly I realized that there is more to life than baseball.

There are also girls!

Even at the age of six, I was beginning to get a funny feeling in my belly whenever women were around. I had so many crushes—delightful first crushes—and I found them in the strangest places.

In the first grade, it was Sister Beatrice.

Sister Beatrice smelled great. I did all I could to figure out ways to get close to her. Shoe-tying was one ritual that required assistance. With high hopes I would offer my leg out.

"Excuse me, Sister, could you please tie my shoes?"

Sister Beatrice would then drop to one knee to help. When she leaned down, I leaned down—all the way. My nose nearly touched her forehead, which peeked out of her hat. She would be too busy to notice, and I would whiff away.

I smelled baby powder. I smelled Ivory soap. I smelled her. She smelled better than my brother's bottom after Mom put a new diaper on him. Being close to her, having her talk di-

Sartorial splendor, first grade at St. Stephen's.

rectly to me, made me swoon. I'd breathe in deeply so that I had some of her smell left over when I went back to my desk.

I loved her.

By the holidays, my grandfather had taught me how to tie a perfect double-knotter, but I never let on.

"Oh, Sister Beatrice, please tie my shoes?"

She started giving me funny looks. By the spring of first grade, every other kid in the class tied his own shoes. I could see it in her eyes. "What's wrong with this boy?"

I had a choice: I could go on letting her think I was a moron, or I could begin tying my own shoes, and lose my best opportunity to smell her. It was no contest.

"Aren't you practicing like I showed you?" Sister Beatrice asked.

"All the time," I said. " I just can't get it. I feel so bad."

I loved Sister Beatrice for another reason. At lunchtime, when they closed off the street to let the kids play in front of the school, she would join our punchball game. On her knees, she'd help us draw the bases on the street, and when she stood up her front would be loaded with chalk. It went well with the chalk on her bottom. In class, she liked to lean against the blackboard while flipping an eraser in one hand. She never dropped it. Not once.

When Sister Beatrice was at bat she would whack the ball, punching it between the fielders. Then she would scoot to first base holding her heavy skirts up with both hands, flying past the parked cars. I would stare at her black wide-heeled nun shoes and black stockings. The shoes were perfect for kicking field goals.

In second grade I became a choirboy. I was no fool— at the time I was one of only two boy sopranos surrounded by blue-skirted girls. Three times a week they stuck me right in the middle of them. I loved their white socks and their black and white shoes. The girls needed to cover their heads with school-issued beanies when they entered the church. If a girl forgot her beanie, she had to think quickly. One day, my all-time crush, Katie O'Dea, forgot her beanie. I moved in.

"Katie, would you like my hankie?"

"Did you blow your nose in it?"

I showed her both sides twice.

"Clean as a whistle, just washed with Clorox."

Katie accepted my hankie. With a bobby pin, she fixed it to her silky black hair. I stood back. She was Bernadette of Lourdes. The only thing missing were the sheep and a couple of farm kids. We were in the choir, high in the back of the low-lit church, but I imagined we were in the French grotto where the Blessed Virgin appeared to Bernadette. With a halo glowing softly over her head, Katie smiled at me and whispered, "Thank you." My knees grew weak.

The hankie stayed in my pocket for three weeks before my mother, a notorious neat freak, noticed me hiding it under my bunk-bed mattress.

She said, "What are doing?"

"Nothing."

She came closer for a look-see.

"What are you, nuts? There's snot all over that thing. Give it to me."

"No, no, I have a cold. I don't want anyone else catching it."

She grabbed it. "I worry about you."

I sighed as my beloved hankie flew through the air, hit the lip of the hamper and slipped beneath the rim into the pile of dirty laundry.

I remained in the choir, buried in the middle of my harem, until that horrible day my voice changed and I reluctantly retired. But I had other schemes cooking at St. Stephen's.

In fourth grade, Sister Adrienne said to me, "One more word, one more word, mister, and you'll be staying after school."

That wasn't a threat. It was an invitation.

I loved being around the nuns, especially after school. They acted differently then. They were regular people, with normal feelings. Figuring out ways to spend more time with them outside of school was easy. I had a big mouth. I was constantly being told to "watch my step."

And if I was punished and had to stay after school, a nun had to stay with me. Forty empty desks, the nun, and me. Perfect.

I learned it could play out three ways. First, she would keep you in the classroom for a long time, then home you went. Second, she gave up and would let you out early. Third, wanting to punish you, but not punish herself, she would have you come with her up to the nuns' residence. I preferred Door No. 3.

One day, Sister Adrienne took me to that mysterious residence on the fifth floor that had curtained windows, but of course no classrooms. I was in the nuns' private sanctuary. She would put me in the study room and tell me to keep my mouth shut. It was heaven. I was so quiet she forgot I was there.

Sometime later, Sister Grace, the principal, came into the study and jumped when she saw me.

"Thomas, what are doing here?"

"I'm not sure. Sister Adrienne put me here."

"Why did she put you here?"

"Oh, I'm being punished for something. She said she was sick of the classroom, so she brought me up here and put me in this room."

"Well, you sitting here like a lump is doing no one any good. Do you want to do something useful?"

"Sure!"

"Come with me."

We went to the kitchen. It was the hugest one I had ever seen.

"Help me with the string beans," she said.

This I knew how to do. Mom always made string beans. All you did was twist off the ends. I jumped up on a tall stool by the wood-block counter and began my chore. Most of the nuns walked through the kitchen at one time or other while I worked away. When Sister Adrienne walked in, she was ready to scold me—it was a no-no for non-nuns to be in the kitchen. But Sister Grace shot her a look that said, "I put the kid to work. Let's leave it at that."

I began mischievously to worm my way into the nuns' residence on a regular basis. Sometimes, my "punishments" included polishing the furniture or vacuuming the rugs. Other times I had to sit in the study and read books about the saints and all the great ways that they had died.

Late one afternoon, Sister Grace popped her head into the study and found me reading with my feet up on a hassock.

"Are you still here?" she asked.

"Well, I was worried you might have something else for me to do," I replied.

"It's almost 5:30!"

"What are you making for dinner?"

"Thomas, go home."

I left slowly, hoping she would change her mind and call me back. In a way, their sanctuary had become a haven for me, too, a place where I could observe these women that I loved—the first women I was ever attracted to—in all their mystery—from a safe distance.

The Girl Who Killed Santa

Deborah spills the beans to me about Santa. When we get to the Macy's Parade, not even Bullwinkle J. Moose of Frostbite Falls, Minnesota can help me.

Thanksgiving morning, 1961. Mom wakes me quietly and whispers, "Rory is sick. If you wake him up before you leave, you're not going either."

I nodded my head yes. I felt bad that my brother wouldn't see the parade, but I was happy to go with Dad alone. It was much easier to have a good time with Dad when it was just the two of us. This was my first Macy's parade and I didn't want one of Dad's bad moods blowing it.

At nine o'clock, we slipped out the door. We met Dad's friend Richie Kovarik and his daughter, Deborah, inside Loftus Tavern a few blocks away. The four of us were going together. Richie was talking to Jack, the bar's owner, over coffee. Deborah sat on a barstool sipping a Coke and sucking a cube of ice with the hole in the middle. She was a year older than I was, stuck up, and knew everything.

I hated her guts.

Richie greeted us. "Hi, Bob. Where's Rory?"

"He's sick. We'll catch up later at my mother's for dinner. Hi, Deborah, you look so pretty and grown up."

With a wide phony smile she said, "Thank you, Mr. Pryor."

I almost vomited.

Saying goodbye to Jack, we went out the bar's side door, smack into a vicious cold wind. A Checker cab was just turning off York Avenue heading west on 85th Street.

"Cabby," Dad yelled and we piled in.

Despite plenty of room to sit alongside our fathers, Deborah and I naturally sat on the round pull-up seats that faced them. That's because for adults a Checker cab was transpor-

The Sailor Man himself, Thanksgiving Parade, 1961.

tation, but for kids it was an amusement ride and the bouncy pull-up seats were why. It was better than most rides, in fact, because there was nothing to strap you in.

Deborah and I didn't acknowledge each other. The cab made it nonstop from York Avenue to Fifth Avenue through a swirl of green and yellow lights. My head slapped the roof several times. The driver impressed me. Crossing Fifth Avenue, we dove into the Transverse through Central Park.

"You're in second grade, right?" Deborah asked.

"Yes."

"I'm in third grade," she said, pleased as punch.

She knew what grade I was in. She continued talking while looking out her window. I tried ignoring her.

"What are you getting for Christmas?" she asked.

That was a dirty trick. It's nearly impossible for a kid to stay silent when this subject comes up.

"Things," I said.

"I'm getting a bike and an Erector set."

"That's nice," I said.

"What did you ask for?" Deborah pressed on.

"I'm still deciding. I have a list."

"What's on the list?"

"Lots of stuff."

"Oh, come on, name a few things."

"That's between me and Santa."

"WHAT?" she asked.

"It's between me and Santa."

"Well, good luck, dummy, because there ain't no Santa."

Despite my lingering hope, I worried that this was true. I wanted her dead.

I tried to recover. "I know there's no Santa, stupid."

"No you didn't, but you do now." Her eyebrows arched up and down.

"I play along for my brother. It makes him feel good. He's just a kid."

"Still believe in the Easter Bunny?" she asked.

"Oh crap, him too?" I thought, then said, "No, of course not."

I never realized until that moment how much detail there was on the stone blocks lining the underpasses through Central Park. The road was twisting and bumpy. My forehead banged repeatedly against the window's glass. It felt good. It took my mind off the other pain. Silently staring out, I saw the glitter of the granite and the chiseled cuts where they had sliced the stone to make the blocks. I imagined Deborah's head being dragged across that rock as we drove back and forth through the park. Kaput!

"Johnny, leave us off on the near corner of 86th and Central Park West," Dad's voice broke into my dream of vengeance.

The driver aimed for the curb. The air was frigid. I barely noticed. Normally, I would've run ahead toward the action, but my heart remained behind on the cab's pull-up seat. I took Dad's hand, even though I didn't feel like a little boy anymore. We walked south to 77th Street in formation. Dad squeezed my hand. I weakly squeezed back.

"I don't think we're staying too long," Dad said to Richie. "I think Tommy's got something, too."

We stood inside the park's wall on the rocks. This allowed us to see the parade over the sidewalk crowd. Only because Dad announced the balloon names as they passed by, do I remember they included Underdog, Popeye, and Bullwinkle J. Moose from Frostbite Falls, Minnesota.

Over the River and Through the Potatoes

*Thanksgiving hijinks: The turkey takes wing, and
Pop Rode's three-note snore inspires a song.*

Around one o'clock on the same day that Deborah spilled the
beans about Santa and the Easter Bunny, Dad and I arrived at
his family's apartment for Thanksgiving dinner. Dad's mom
and his stepdad, John Rode (also called Nan and Pop, just
like our other grandparents) always cooked our bird. Mom's
parents did the Easter lamb roast. At the kitchen table, Mom
and Nan Rode were snapping the ends off a few pounds of
string beans and throwing them into a spaghetti pot. Rory
and Pop were in the living room watching *Babes in Toyland,*
starring Laurel and Hardy.

"Hi, all," Dad said. "I thought we were eating at one?"

"The bird's got a way to go—maybe another hour," Nan
said.

Mom gave Dad a silent "no way."

Dad went over to the oven and opened the front.

"Jesus Christ, who are you feeding?"

"Shut your mouth," Nan said.

"That prehistoric beast is the same size as Rory," Dad said.

"Mind your business."

"Did the tribe bring him down with a spear or a net?" Dad
said.

Mom whispered to me, "Rory is smaller."

"We'll eat tomorrow," Dad said.

"Another hour—go inside and be useful," Nan said, waving Dad away. "Get two folding chairs and bring me my bag.
I forgot something and need you to go to the store."

Dad eyed me up and down. He wanted to send me to the
store but he thought I was getting sick. Resigned, he exhaled

"Nice flash, Bob!" The Pryors dine with the Rodes, 1955.

loudly, ensuring that everyone in the balcony knew he was leaving the stage.

I was glum after my encounter with Deborah, but being at Nan's was cheering me up. Everything was big. She was big. Pop was big. The coffee cups were big. At her house, I could drink anything I wanted when I wanted.

Dad returned from the front room to the kitchen with Nan's pocketbook. I could see his arm muscles working hard, lifting the heavy bag.

"Here you go. What do you need?" Dad said.

"Go down to Parker's and get me a pound of butter."

Dad walked to the fridge, opened the door and stuck his head in it. "You have a full pound."

"I need six sticks for the mashed potatoes."

"We're six people! That's a quarter pound of butter per person. Are you trying to stop our hearts with a single meal?"

"I'm making mashed potatoes for the week and it's none of your business. Get the butter."

"And the thirty-pound bird? I suppose that's part of your long-term meal plan?"

"Don't exaggerate. It's twenty-six pounds."

"Oh, only twenty-six pounds. Let's see, at more than four pounds per person that should cover our meat provision on our Easter Island sea voyage."

I was curious: Would Nan slap him or not? I was pulling for a slap. She seemed real close. Instead, she stared him down. He wisely took the money and went to the grocery store.

About an hour after his return he said to Nan, "I'm starving. How much longer?"

"I'll take a look."

I watched through the doorway. Nan opened the oven and took the turkey out, firmly hanging on to both pan handles. From behind, she looked like a Russian Olympic weightlifter. She placed the pan on the counter and checked the thermometer. Dad was right behind her.

"What does it say?" Dad said.

"135 degrees," Nan said.

"Forget it, put it back in."

"No, it's done."

"You're nuts."

"It's fine. Look."

Nan sliced into the meat. It was pink as a flower.

"Meat is supposed to be 175 degrees before you eat it," Dad said. "That bird just stopped breathing."

"That's it, let's go," Nan said and moved the enormous pan toward the table. Dad met her halfway and began guiding her back toward the oven. They both had their hands on the pan's small handles.

A turkey dance!

"Give it to me," Dad said.

"Leave me alone," Nan said. "Start mashing the potatoes."

"Give it to me!"

He tugged. She tugged. The pan didn't know what to do.

So it flipped over. The bird leaped to its death with all its natural juices, landing on Dad's new dress shoes with the little pinholes all over the leather. Stunned, Nan and Dad stared down at the linoleum and the bird for a long time. Nan spoke first.

"Ah shit, I'm lying down." And she did.

She passed through the living room. I was frozen in the doorway and Pop had Rory on his lap. They watched like two largemouth bass. Then Mom joined Rory watching TV and Pop went to the kitchen and began to help Dad. They put the bird back in the pan with a couple of cups of water to replace the lost gravy. Then they put the pan back in the oven. Dad's clothes were splattered with turkey juice, so Pop gave him one of his extra-large T-shirts. None of Pop's pants fit Dad, so he gave Dad a pair of boxer shorts. Dad wore Pop's boxers over his own boxers—all in all a nice picture with his dark socks and skinny legs. I saw Mom peek in and start to laugh.

Sometime much later, Pop announced, "OK, everything is ready."

He went into the front room and brought Nan back. She returned to the kitchen and took over as if nothing had happened.

"Bob, carve the meat."

Dad grabbed the knife and did as he was told. This relieved everyone. The table comfortably sat six people yet with the large amount of food on it, it was hard for us to see each other. Everyone was scary polite. Late in the meal, Dad looked at the bucket of mashed potatoes and said, "You know from this angle, I believe I can see a couple of goats circling the top of Potato Mountain."

We all laughed except Nan. But she didn't hit him. The storm passed and Rory and I started looking forward to our favorite Thanksgiving ritual—Pop-watching. He was a gentle bear and never yelled at us. After the meal, he drank two short glasses of Ballantine Ale, wiped his mouth carefully with his linen napkin, and said, "Thank you, and excuse me."

He lifted himself from the table, and walked from his kitchen chair to his living room chair. Once Rory and I heard

"Swoosh"—Pop's bottom sinking into the plastic—we started counting backward, "10-9-8-7-6-5-4-3-2-1..."

We peeked into the living room. Pop was asleep. Rory and I stared at him.

Then a cartoon came onto the TV about two poor kids who go to bed with nothing to eat. They dream, people come and bring them goodies, and music begins to play. Rory and I stood behind Pop's chair, one on each side of his head, and sang quietly into his ears along with the cartoon song:

Meet me tonight in dreamland, under the silvery moon.
Meet me tonight in dreamland, where love's sweet roses
    bloom.
Come with the love light gleaming, in your dear eyes
    of blue.
Meet me in dreamland, sweet dreamy dreamland,
There let my dreams come true.

Our singing didn't wake him. Pop had a stretched-out snore with three different sounds. And Nan had a toy piano with eight color-coded keys. You could play a full octave of tones. The piano came with a color-coded music book with classics like "Pop Goes the Weasel," "Roll Out the Barrel," and "This Old Man." Rory was pretty good on the thing—he played "Jingle Bells" with ease—and soon he went over to it. In between Pop's snores he'd hit a key. He played around a bit until he located a couple of notes that harmonized with Pop's snoring.

Not wanting to be left out, and not having Rory's natural musical talent, I improvised. Nan's toilet door made a creaking sound, so I opened it a smidge to see if I could somehow join the band. I found a funky "eek" and added it to the mix. Leaning over, looking back into the living room, I could see Rory. Once we made eye contact, it was easy to find our rhythm. We riffed, "Snore, piano key, eek; snore, piano key, eek."

"Our song had a hook," as Dad liked to say. Mom, who had moved into the kitchen, threw a sponge at my head. I ducked. The band played on. Sponge two was in the air. I avoided it by doing the cha-cha.

"I will kill you both," she said. "Keep it up and I'll kill you both."

Noticing that Mom had run out of sponges, and the next airborne item could be a spoon or a fork, Rory and I left the airwaves. Dad moved to the sink area to join Mom. I sat on the washing machine right next to them. Mom picked up a dish and started scrubbing. Dad squeezed too much dish soap into the water, and then began to play with the faucet's screws.

"Let's get this over with," Mom said. "You're moping."

"Not true, the secret is a long hot soak," Dad said. "Then the grease slides itself off." He continued to play with the faucet.

"The secret is you're full of shit and have a bony ass," Mom said.

Two Guys
Talking on the Corner

It's movie night. With a little help from Mr. Peabody's time-travel machine, I stare Dad down for the first time.

Dad and I did four things together: play sports, attend sports, watch TV, and go to the movies. I liked movies the best; it's much harder telling a kid what to do in the dark. You would have loved taking me to the movies when I was 6 years old. I was a cheap date, one box of Pom Poms caramels and a dime soda kept me blissful through the whole film and I shut up. Didn't want to miss anything.

It was fall 1960, I had just started first grade, and I still believed my father was infallible. He never had to use this line on me—"Are you gonna believe what you see or what I tell you?" He accomplished his goals without direct engagement. Looking back, I suspect he periodically forgot I was his son and thought I was the most intelligent dog in the world. But this day would be different.

Dad's charm was in full swing as he pulled me up 86th Street to go the movies. I kept my eye out for friends. The last thing I needed were the guys giving me the business, "Daddy still holds ya hand, Tommy the baby!" Resistance was futile, so I decided to keep tight to Dad's side so it looked like we were just walking very close together.

"So, what do you want to see?" Dad stopped at the corner of Third Avenue, removed the cigarette from his mouth and looked down at me. "*The Mouse that Roared*, a very funny comedy, or the other film up there, *The Time Machine*?"

Up ahead of us on the north side of 86th Street were two movie houses, the Loew's Orpheum and the gigantic RKO.

"What are they about?"

Dad needling me,
Patchogue, summer, 1962.

"Well. . .*The Mouse That Roared* is about a tiny little country that declares war on the United States. The star of the film, Peter Sellers, is a famous English comedian. You'll love him."

I just stared at Dad hoping he'd move on. I didn't like war. Finally he said, "*The Time Machine* is a science fiction movie I don't know much about."

"What do you know?"

"It's about time travel."

"I want to see *The Time Machine*."

Dad stared down at me, holding the look, hoping I'd keep talking. I didn't. Getting this look made me nervous and I usually blabbed on just like Dad wanted so he could carefully talk me out of something. But this time we just stared at each other.

After a pause so long we missed crossing the light, Dad asked, "What?"

"I love time travel."

Dad rolled his eyes. He had no clue how crazy I was for Mr. Peabody and Sherman on *The Rocky and Bullwinkle Show*, which I watched faithfully every Sunday. Mr. Peabody invented the WABAC machine (pronounced "way back"), that allowed him and Sherman to time-travel to ancient Rome, the voyages of Columbus, the dinosaur era—you name it. I wasn't sure what science fiction was, but I loved time travel.

Dad recovered. "Oh, I bet it's going to be one of those talky films you hate."

I said nothing.

Dad threw a wild punch, hoping it would land. "If we go to *The Mouse That Roared* I'll take you to Prexy's afterward for a hamburger and a milk shake."

I ducked his shot. "Why can't we go to Prexy's anyway?"

Dad's shoulders rolled forward and his chest fell as he grabbed my hand. Swiftly, we crossed Third Avenue, sidestepping the spray from a street-cleaner truck, and headed to the RKO to see Rod Taylor, whoever he was, in *The Time Machine*.

The Third Beer

Timing is everything when I ask Dad and his drinking pals to take me to Yankee Stadium. The sweet spot: between the third and fourth beers, when normally dismissed suggestions become done deeds.

I barehanded the Spaldeen off the wall.

"Nice catch, Tommy," Dad said.

"Thanks," I answered.

We continued our ritual—Dad on the south side of 85th Street and me on the north side. We played outside Loftus Tavern. Loftus, where my Dad had danced on the bar the night I was born.

He threw high ones off the wall, teaching me how to play Fenway Park's left field. If I was going to play for the Yankees, I had to conquer the "Green Monster," the most treacherous wall in baseball.

I described the action to the fans. "Oh my! Tommy makes a shoestring catch, whirls, and fires a strike to second base, robbing Carl Yastrzemski of a double."

"Last throw," Dad said.

The ball flew over my head. I turned and put my hand up to where I thought it would be.

"Got it."

Dad ran across the street and gave me a hug. Our catches never ended on a dropped ball.

Arm in arm, we entered the tavern, where the air conditioner buzzed over our heads. The mingling of my sweat with the chill delighted me. Our thirst was deep.

It was July 1961. I had a dime in my dungaree pocket. I put Johnny Cash on the jukebox and draped my body over so the bass rumbled through my belly.

After the song, I climbed onto a barstool alongside Dad. Jack Loftus brought us a beer and a Coke—our usual. The

Dad, Allie, and Mickey on York Avenue.

newspapers were spread over the bar. I grabbed *The Daily News* and dug into the sports pages. There were three other customers—Dad's friends, Gene and Allie, and my Uncle Mickey.

Perfect.

I hurled my first salvo. "Ford's pitching today and going for his tenth straight win. Imagine that, old Whitey going for ten straight before the All-Star break!"

Gene and Allie's ears perked up. They loved Ford.

"Chairman of the Board," they said with hushed respect each time his name was mentioned.

My next target was Mickey.

"Wow, Mantle and Maris are both ahead of Ruth's home run pace. The way they're slugging the ball, they both could break the record."

Mickey's eyes left his newspaper. He knew I loved Mantle.

"They better do it in 154 games," he said. "Otherwise, the record may not count."

"Will too," I said.

"We'll see. There's a rumor that the baseball commissioner will give the record an asterisk if it happens after the 154th game."

I had no clue what an asterisk was—but whatever it was, I didn't want one next to Mantle's name. I glared at my uncle. He smirked.

But I didn't pursue the matter because I had an agenda today: These guys were taking me to Yankee Stadium to watch Whitey Ford beat the Boston Red Sox.

I knew I had to ask at the right time. Too soon would be before the third beer. Somewhere between the third and fourth beer, euphoria took grown men to a place where most normally dismissed suggestions became done deeds.

Too late would be at any point after the fourth beer. They'd be settled in and lazy, and the thought of going back out into the heat would keep them in the bar all afternoon.

The third beer was served—I waited until each took a sip.

"Hey guys, when was the last time we went up to the Bronx together? Wasn't it the Indians the day before Mother's Day? We gotta see the old ballpark; catch some sun in the bleachers? Whaddaya say?"

My tanning reference was aimed at my handsome uncle.

Everyone exchanged looks. I put on my pathetic face. Dad paused for a moment, then shook his head and said, "You're a real piece of work."

He rubbed my dirt-brown crew cut, pushed off his barstool, and slapped both hands on the bar.

"Let's go, men. Chairman Ford needs our support. Jack, save our seats."

**Ready to clobber one
in Central Park.**

We rose together and drained our drinks. Jack cleared the glasses and the cardboard Rheingold coasters off the wet bar. He swept it dry with one long ride of his rag.

"Have a great time, men," Jack said, winking at me. He leaned over the bar and whispered, "Nice job, Tommy."

Out in the street, the heat smacked us in the face. A Checker cab flew towards us. Fearing a retreat if there was any delay, I yelled "CAB-BAY." We piled in and Dad said, "Johnny, Yankee Stadium."

Unbelievable, he did it again! Dad knew every cab driver's name—and they were all Johnnies.

We raced up the FDR Drive with all the windows rolled down. I sat on the East River side of the cab with my head sticking out the window, catching air in my mouth. Done with that, I began singing beer jingles, getting in the mood for the game, "Baseball and Ballantine," started us off.

The men joined in on the next number, "Schaefer Is the One Beer to Have When You're Having More Than One."

The pull-up seats built into a Checker's floor resembled toilet bowls with no opening to do your business. It was my favorite amusement ride. I flew around the space like a bottle cap in an empty clothes dryer. Trips were rated by the number of times my head smacked the roof. Eleven. This was a good one.

The driver dropped us off under the El on River Avenue. A train roared over our heads. I looked up at the large green sign, "Bleachers 75 cents." I held Dad's hand tight. I didn't want to lose him. Going through the turnstile entrance, we moved into near darkness under the outfield seats. Dad bought me a program and a pencil. I ran ahead with Allie toward the sunshine and into the bleachers. We found a spot against the bullpen fence. All around, people were laughing and screaming at each other. I took particular notice of certain words. Words I vaguely understood, but knew I could never say in front of an adult. Allie had his eye on me while I absorbed the colorful language.

"Hey kid, how old are you?"

"I'm seven."

Allie put his arm around me and said, "Well, pardner, when you leave here today you'll be eighteen."

Out of the corner of my eye, I noticed Dad playing with his lips trying to hide a smile.

I carefully wrote the starting lineups in my program in neat block letters.

Finishing, I lifted my head and saw Gene talking down into the Yankee bullpen.

"Dad, who is Gene talking to?"

"Luis Arroyo."

"Huh?"

"Luis Arroyo, the All-Star pitcher. Gene and Arroyo played together in the minors ten years ago."

"Gene knows Luis Arroyo?"

"Yep, they were roommates for two seasons."

I had no words. Dad's friend was the ex-roommate of the Yankee who happened to be the best relief pitcher in baseball? This fact slipped his mind? Is this what happens when you turn 32?

"Hey, Tommy." I turned and saw Gene waving me over to the bullpen. I gulped and inched toward him. Standing next to Gene, I looked down at the ballplayer. He spoke to me.

"Hi, Tommy, it's a pleasure to meet you."

"Hi, Mr. Arroyo."

"Call me Luis."

The ballplayer passed two fingers through the tightly meshed fence. That's all that fit. I offered him my two fingers. He started laughing.

"Gene, put the kid over the fence."

Gene, six-foot-four, lifted me, four-foot-nothing, over the bullpen fence into the arms of the Yankee pitcher. His powerful hands eased me down. My heart pounded, my legs shook. I felt loopy. Luis introduced me to three Yankees—Yogi Berra, Johnny Blanchard, and Hector Lopez. They towered over me. Whitey Ford, warming up, waved and smiled. Whitey Ford smiled at me.

It's hard to remember the players' faces. I was dumbstruck by the giant interlocking NY on their pinstripe uniforms. My eyes moved from one jersey to another, rarely leaving the insignia. I thought I knew every sound in the ballpark—Bob Shepherd's splendid voice over the stadium's loudspeaker, "In center field...number seven...Mickey Mantle...number seven." The vendors hawking, "BEER HERE, GET YOUR ICE COLD BEER HERE—BEER! A ball hitting the web of a glove, "WOOF!" A line drive foul striking an empty wooden seat: "THWACK!"

But in the bullpen I heard fresh sounds. Like the players' voices, direct and unfiltered by the radio or TV. The sound of their steel cleats scraping against the gravel and concrete bullpen floor, "Scritch, scritch, scritch." I placed those sounds in my memory vault.

How did the game turn out? *Of course I remember!*

Ford won his tenth straight. Luis saved the game for Whitey, striking out five of the last six batters. Mantle hit his 29th home run in the fifth inning.

Final score: Yankees 8, Red Sox 5.

Beans in My Pocket

When a nun demands that you finish your kidney beans,
forming them into a cross might be a smart bid for mercy.
Or it might not.

"John, what did you do with the egg?" I worked the words out of the side of my mouth.

"It's in my pocket," John said.

"Are you sure the egg is safe?"

"Yes, you idiot."

Our squawking drew Sister Adrienne's attention. As the lunch hour wound down, the nuns put a collar on talking. The more you yapped the longer it took them to force you to finish your crappy food.

"John and Thomas, put a lid on it. You have two minutes, two minutes misters, to finish everything. Do you hear me?"

"Yes, Sister."

John, from across the table mouthed a silent, "You're dead, stupid."

I made a face back. I thought that the nun was behind me... Wrong.

"Young man, was that face intended for me?

"No."

"Do you think this is a joke?"

"No, no, no, Sister. I have allergies and sometimes I scratch the inside of my nose by moving my face around. This is good in case it itches when my hands aren't free."

Sister Adrienne let out a long exhale that caved her chest in.

"Well you both can sit there until the ice skating rink is done in Hell. There are poor children starving in China. You dwell on that."

John gave me a nasty look. I returned one. I was positive that a part of a nun's final exam involved convincing the

Shipshape tie. Is it a clip-on?

mother superior that the candidate truly believed there was a connection between kids finishing what was left on their plates and fewer kids starving worldwide.

John had the egg in his pocket because he had no intention of eating it, and he couldn't leave the basement cafeteria until his tray was cleared. I daydreamed about my mother's punishment for forcing me into the school lunch program.

Mom did the math a week after Rory entered first grade and I started third grade. She was losing two hours picking up her, "two pain in the asses," taking us home, feeding us, and then returning us to school as we fought along the way. Our lack of defense put the both of us into the program, or as the older kids called it, " The Pain Meal Plan." You could not bring your own lunch to school. The parish, greedy for profit, wanted to lift lunch enrollment. They hired an old lady in the 1930s that everyone called "Ma" to cook for 150 kids. Her specialties: boiled green meat and extra-rotten celery in all unidentifiable soups.

While John settled his egg into his pants, I rearranged the cold kidney beans on my plate for the sixth time. The smiley face was gone. The beans now formed a crucifix. Sister Adrienne could take this a few ways. My preference was that she admire that I was thinking about Our Lord while we were passing this time together. She went another way and saw my bean work as further proof of my defiance. She loved that word.

"Thomas, your defiance will lead you to ruin. Not only will you not get out of here to play with the other children, but if you don't finish the beans and the sandwich on your plate, you will stay after school."

Sister Adrienne's foot kept time throughout her speech. Watching her shoe tap reminded me of a hoedown. I pictured her in a straw hat, overalls, checkered shirt, and red kerchief telling everyone in the barn, "Well swing your partner and do-si-do." Then I moaned, thinking about my classmates playing box ball in front of the school.

"Sister, I'm not feeling well. This is the best I can do."

"Bite it, chew it."

"This is not meat."

John whispered to me, "I love it."

The sandwich had a plug of greenish-brown ham that was thick enough to sit in front of Snoopy's doghouse as a doormat. Its curled dry edges, sticking out of the stale wheat bread, was a certified vomit starter. I gave up on salvaging the remaining lunchtime but had no intention of staying after school. It was 70 degrees and sunny. The park was screaming for me to get over there.

Back at the gulag, strange John loved cold beans and thick chunks of ham. He even showed me every half-chewed bite in his mouth, dropping his jaw all the way down to give me a bird's eye view of his progress. His eyes stayed on the nun and followed her around—when she looked at him his mouth closed shut. After his final swallow and an audible "aaahhh," he gave me a smile, a head motion towards his empty plate, wiggled his eyebrows and bid me farewell.

"See ya, numb nuts."

John held his red tray up for presentation to the nun. I wanted to kick him in the ass. While the sister looked John over, I slipped a handful of white beans into my pocket and rushed back to my fork. I had no opportunity to put the beans in anything, so they gooked up in my pants.

With John gone, it was the nun and me. She moved over to give me her full attention.

"You've made some progress."

I smiled, sensing something behind her stone eyes. "Yes, Sister, I've done all I can."

I tried a pathetic look here, going for Dondi, the Italian orphan from the Sunday comics.

"Can I go now?"

A glint of kindness muscled its way round her iron mask.

"You can leave the rest of the beans, but you must finish the sandwich."

She might as well have told me, "You don't have to jump off the building, but I am still setting you on fire."

I mashed the remaining beans for good luck and centered the sandwich. I imagined it was a hot dog. It was hopeless. The scary odor coming from the pretend meat closed off all avenues of self-trickery.

I stared down at the black plague. I was ready to wait until the Pope had a baby. At one o'clock we'd be due to line up in front of the school to return to class. Sister Adrienne gave up torturing me. We took turns looking at each other, looking at the clock, looking at the sandwich, and looking at our feet. Did you know that the second hand on a clock doesn't just circle around without stopping? No, no, it stops at each second with a little jerk. Nuggets like that kept me going until loud shoes smacking the wood floor interrupted my daydreaming. I looked up and saw Father Edward.

"Excuse me, Sister Adrienne, I thought lunch was over."

"It should be."

"Sister, I can come back a little later."

"No, Father Edward, please take care of your business."

"No, that's OK, thank you." The priest left.

Sister's eyes followed his shadow long after he left the room.

She liked the priest. Everyone knew that. Father Edward was an ex-Marine chaplain and still exercised. While she eyed Father Edward I thought of balling the sandwich and putting it in my pocket. I decided against it. She would probably pat me down on the way out. A word popped up in my mind: margarine. There was enough of it on the bread to stucco a wall. I slipped the two sandwich pieces apart and made sure the meat was stuck solid to the bread and that the top of the meat was swimming in margarine. Then I pressed the wet sides firmly to the bottom of the table. They squished. It felt horrible. Sister Adrienne turned back toward me. I chewed on the imaginary last wad of phony pig in my mouth. She didn't believe me for a second.

I faked a swallow and got up to show her my tray. She patted me down while looking around to see if she missed something. As I left the lunchroom, I heard her mumbling behind me. I headed to the boys' room to dump the beans and the egg I had stuck in my pocket. I threw them into the bowl on top of John's unflushed egg. School lunch was killing me.

Nan's Star Boarder

My grandmother loves me to death.
She also treats me like her farm animal.

I was five years old, sitting on Nan Rode's toilet bowl and nearing an important decision. My feet were asleep. I liked that feeling. If they were a little asleep I could hop off and stand on my own. If they were a lot asleep I was going to fall. If I went one way, not too bad. I'd hit the plaster wall and work my way up as the feeling came back into my legs. The other way, not too good. I pushed my bottom forward to stand. . . .

Boom.

My moonshot, with Nan and Rory, 1956.

71

I whacked the door to my left, striking the ironing board hanging from its hook. The door flew open and hit the china closet as my body smacked the linoleum with a thud.

"What the hell was that?" My grandmother's voice roared from the front room.

I heard her yelling, but what could I do? My legs were sawed off, no longer part of my body. As Nan got closer, I lay there rubbing my thighs. There was a horseshoe over the apartment's front door, but that day it wasn't doing me much good.

A shadow filled my sky. Nan was a big lady and she was leaning in. I smelled Jean Naté.

"What did I tell you?"

I tried to answer but all that came out of my mouth were whiny moans. "Mmmm, ooh, ooh."

"You're mumbling. I told you to do your business in there and get out. Until you grow taller, and your feet touch the floor, everything in there is one-two-three. Pull up your underwear and put your bird away."

That I was lying on the floor, a crumpled cripple begging to be healed, was meaningless to her. I had disrupted her housecleaning schedule. She gave all her attention to clearing the accident scene to get the traffic rolling again. I felt the cars going around me. I did as she said. I rarely pushed my luck with Nan. My heinie had a long memory.

Nan was neat, but in her own way. As her sometime farm animal and apprentice, I quickly learned that she had a special touch when it came to housekeeping.

Her floor-through railroad flat was immaculate in three of its four rooms. The fourth was the junk room. To navigate it, even a kid had to watch his shoulders. Dad called it the "Northwest Passage." Most households did an annual spring-cleaning. My grandmother's cleaning schedule had four seasons. Every three months, everything moved. Things came out and things got put away, packed into the four gigantic black metal closets in the junk room, each of which was topped off by a large cardboard storage box with flowers printed on them. Many boxes were held together with duct tape. The only other piece of furniture in the room was the flattest, most uncomfortable couch on earth.

"A fat family in the circus owned the couch," Mom said. "They sold it to a prison. Nan picked it up cheap at a rummage sale."

When I was bad, the couch was my punishment. I had to sit there until I was good, or until Nan needed me to help with a chore. The naked light bulb and the four monster closets still creep into my nightmares now and then. I'm sure that space prompted my deep claustrophobia. I couldn't breathe in there. Dad told me his middle brother, Charlie, went into the junk room when he was seven years old and never came back.

"Vanished," Dad said.

Everything in that room at some point was called a "whatchamacallit." I learned to cover my head when I opened one of the closet doors. Each time I did, the Marx Brothers stowaway scene reappeared in my brain. Instead of people tumbling on me, out came the whatchamacallits. Shoeboxes, curtains, tablecloths, doilies, mothballs, comforters, plastic zipped-up quilt bags, and hatboxes. I ducked flying knitting needles as balls of multicolored wool unraveled over me. Plastic quart bottles bounced off my noggin.

These disasters began innocently enough. I'd be in the front bedroom reading a comic book. From two rooms away I'd hear, "Tommy!"

"What?"

"Go into closet No. 2 and get the large white box that says 'Grand Street' on the side."

Nan taped numbers on the closets.

I'd open the closet and be the guest of honor at an inanimate-object surprise party. Once I stopped ducking, Nan and I played a game.

"What's going on in there?"

"I didn't do anything. It all fell out."

"Be careful. I have everything in order."

"You big liar," I thought, but said, "Well, there are no white boxes in the front. There's only one big hatbox."

"Move it."

I moved it.

"There's nothing behind it."

I was stuck behind enemy lines. Nan continued to boss me around the junk room from afar, until I found the item behind one of the whatchamacallits. I have no memory of Nan and me ever being in the same room, at the same time, looking for something. Nan treated the junk room and me like farm animals. We had our purpose, and knew our jobs.

* * *

One Saturday when I was eight, I used my shoulder to pop the ancient vestibule door with the barely working lock and ran up the stairs into her apartment.

"It's me," I yelled into the living room.

Nan, stretched out on her couch, yelled back. "Hi, Tommy."

"Hi, Nan."

"How'd you get in?"

"Someone let me in."

"You didn't pop the door?"

"No."

"Are you hungry?"

"Yeah!" I licked my lips.

"How would you like a big fat juicy hamburger?"

My heart skipped a beat. "Sure!"

"Well, when you make yourself one, make me one, too."

I stepped into the kitchen for my first cooking lesson. The chef barked directions from the living room to her young apprentice.

"Use the large black frying pan."

"Put the flame all the way up."

"Make two big patties."

"Use all the meat."

"Put butter in the pan."

"Be generous."

"Open the windows wide and turn on the fan."

"Make sure the fan is blowing out."

After nearly losing a finger through the grill, I was sure the fan was blowing out. A column of smoke rose in a steady plume toward the white tin ceiling. A minute passed.

"How you doing?"

"Just turned them over."

"Good. Now leave them alone for a minute. Go to the drawer and get the big knife. Get the rye bread and cut four slices."

The blade looked like a shark.

After a long pause, Nan added, "Be careful with the knife. Watch your other hand while you cut. Make sure you use the sharp side. Don't be stingy with the slices. Cut 'em big."

When Nan was hungry, her few kitchen rules flew out the window. Anything that contributed to getting the food to the table more quickly was encouraged. This was a pleasant relief from Mom, who mumbled obscenities if I stepped into the kitchen after she was done cleaning up.

Nan loved meat rare. But when I cooked that first time the frying pan reached temperatures rarely seen outside a foundry. The color of the ceiling over the stove turned a rich mix of black, brown and dirty white swirls.

When the burgers were done, I served Nan on the couch. I opened a snack table so we could eat together. In between chews, Nan looked up at me and said, "Good job." I smiled and bit into my reward.

After burgers, I moved on to grilled cheese and then to skirt steak cooked in the broiler, a magical meat with explosive grease smacks. By nine, I had acquired the culinary skills of a seasoned short-order cook: a combination of my grandmother's trust in me and her utter disregard for grease fires and my well-being.

Nan also taught me how to shop. Every time I went to the store, Nan carefully measured my purchases. In football, there is an expression, "You're only as good as your last pass." Fans and some grandmothers are fickle and want results on every play. With Nan, every time I left the house to do a chore I expected and received justice, not mercy.

She would send me off with a detailed list of items. Before leaving, I received a briefing on each item and vague directions on where I was permitted to exercise flexible judgment. Vegetable and fruit buying were the worst. I knew string beans, I knew carrots, and I knew iceberg lettuce. That was it. If the item had variations in texture or color that required judgment, like pears, apples and peppers, I became a befuddled stranger in a strange land.

Returning from the market, I'd muscle the bags up the stairs into Nan's kitchen, where she'd meet me at the door.

"Put the bags on the table and start rotating the stock. Let's get this show on the road."

Nan's organizational skills were legendary. I was expected to bring all older items forward in the refrigerator and cabinets to make way for the new purchases in the rear. Nan called me her star boarder but the room, soap, and towel were not free. First thing, Nan checked the math on the side of the bags. The grocer used a large black pencil to run the item prices down one side and finish in a second column. If there was an error, back I'd go. She weighed her cold cuts and meats on the 1896 produce scale from her family's fruit stand on York Avenue. This was another go-back issue, but Nan did that one herself.

She'd say, "That son of a bitch. Who does he think he is?" And off she'd go. This rarely happened, but if it happened twice, the store was cut off for good. Nan was feared and respected by the neighborhood merchants. That felt good. I liked having other members in my club.

After completing the math check, Nan sat at the kitchen table and began a running commentary as she emptied the brown bags. My responsibilities at that point were complex. I had to listen to Nan and respond to her questions while moving around the kitchen to get to the right location. That's because, after Nan had examined an item and was satisfied with its price, ripeness, and expiration date, she would throw it in the direction of where it had to go. It was up to me to arrive on time to greet the flying object. I had to measure the velocity, shape and type of object heading my way. Nan did nothing carefully other than crochet and knit. Due to an errant throw, she once put a frozen chocolate chip cookie log through a Tiffany lamp knockoff hanging over the kitchen table.

Though this routine was stressful, no other activity prepared me as well to become the competent football receiver I remain today. The process went like this.

"I see Junket custard was on sale and you bought six boxes, good boy!"

Through the air toward the pantry closet, six small cardboard boxes came at my head. I brought my hands up to protect my face and, I hoped, to catch them.

"Tommy, you only bought one quart. I wrote down two. This milk expires in four days. Did you check in the back of the refrigerator for fresher milk?"

"I did. You know it's Sunday. Tomorrow they get fresh milk. I'll pick up more tomorrow after school."

"OK, now you're cooking with gas," Nan said as she sent the quart of milk rotating to my right. I rescued it before it hit the window behind the washing machine.

"Are these the best bananas they had? They're rocks."

I needed a recovery lie here. I thought hard was good. "I asked Murray to pick them out; he said these were the best he had."

Murray was home sick that day, but I was under pressure.

"Well I'm going to have a talk with Mr. Murray Parker next time I see him."

In rare, peaceful moments at Nan's house, I played in her tiny toilet. It was my private telephone booth. Sitting on the bowl, I thought I was in a space capsule. If I put my left arm up, my elbow hit the door. If I put my right arm up, I'd hit the wall. My knees made contact with a small series of lopsided and wobbly shelves. When I stood up after finishing my business I might instinctively grab one of the shelves to help me into the upright position. Not a good idea.

Since the shelves were inches from my face, it was difficult to hold my comic book properly so I spent time studying bathroom products. I'd read labels on stuff or count the cotton balls in the glass jar. I'd take them all out, count them and put them back in. If one fell in the toilet, I'd pick it out of the water and put it back in the jar. I figured by the time Nan needed to use it, the wet cotton ball would be dry.

When I wasn't memorizing product information, I played with the wool poodles that politely covered the rolls of toilet paper. Nan knitted them for everybody in the neighborhood. It was nice to go to my friends' houses, visit their bathrooms, and see my Nan's poodles there.

Nan's toilet had an old-fashioned water tank high over the bowl with a pull-chain flush. Using the water pipe, I'd climb up over the top of the tank, wedge myself in and float my toy boats on the tank's water. I'd lean down and pull the chain and cause a whirlpool that dragged my ships down to their watery graves. The hole at the bottom of the tank was too small to suck the toys in, so when the tank refilled they popped right back up and started sailing again. "Anchors aweigh, my boys, anchors aweigh."

To the right of the toilet was a small sink and the bathtub, and between them and the toilet door was a large china closet placed sideways flush against the wall to block the view when you took a bath. Nan made Dad nail up a gigantic steel dispenser for wax paper, paper towels and tin foil on the open end of the china closet. Nan stood ready for every conceivable leftover situation. The thing stuck way out with sharp edges like shark fins. The kitchen layout made it impossible to go through the area without hitting a chair, the table or the dispenser. It was bump and bleed. Mom called the dispenser, "The Blood Bank."

Once, when Dad, Nan, and I were watching Lawrence Welk in the living room, Nan felt hungry.

"Bob, get me an apple out of the refrigerator."

Dad grumbled his way out of his living room chair and walked into the kitchen where Mom was playing solitaire at the table. I heard a bump, a shirt tear, and an "ouch" immediately followed by a "shit!"

I leaned toward the doorway and saw Dad holding his upper left arm and Mom laughing.

"What happened?" Nan said.

"Bob go boom," Mom said, continuing to giggle.

Dad gave her the look, got an apple out of the refrigerator, dropped it in Nan's lap and disappeared into the front room holding his arm. He returned with a bandaged arm and a roll of duct tape. When he was done taping the dispenser's edges, there was hardly any metal showing.

I spent many nights at Nan's. If she was awake, noise was good. But if she was asleep, quiet! If I scratched my eye she'd pop up like Dracula. "What was that?"

"Nothing. I'm itching my eye."

After my grandfather died, Nan let me sleep in his bed, alongside her bed. I missed Pop, but knew he didn't want me sleeping on the punishment couch. I practiced keeping still, so Nan would leave me alone. Lying on my back one night, I studied the cracks in the ceiling, and fell asleep imagining what countries they looked like.

"Tommy, Tommy, wake up."

"What's the matter?"

"I heard a noise. Did you do something?"

"I did nothing."

She listened carefully, paused, then said, "Never mind, go back to sleep."

Nan put her head back down on the pillow. I heard her laughing low and then my nose caught an aroma that could down a rogue elephant and flatten a village. Nan had released the "Kraken," farting herself awake and leaving me, her hostage, to die a horrible death.

The Headlock That Won for the Giants

Mom hates people touching her head. But the Giants are down by four points, with less than a minute to go.

Mom crushed indoor horseplay. If Rory and I started in, Mom yelled once. If we continued wrestling, she'd throw things. If we kept it up, she'd hurl us into the hallway outside our apartment and not let us back in until she felt like it. How much time we spent there depended on her mood and the neighbors' complaints.

Mom made one horseplay exception: New York Giants football home games. The National Football League blacked out local TV broadcasts of home games to encourage ticket sales. This remains the most diabolical punishment ever devised to torment me.

By 1964, when I was ten, I had memorized all forty Giant players' numbers, weights, heights, positions, and colleges. I gladly wore my Catholic school uniform, which kept me in Giant blue all week.

Dad went to most Giant home games. If he couldn't swindle a ticket, he'd drive to Connecticut with friends. They'd rent a motel room and watch the game on a station outside the blacked-out area.

On one home game morning, Dad tried sneaking out of the house. I lassoed his leg with my crossed arms.

"Dad, please, please, please."

"Tommy, if I could, I would."

"I'll cheer quietly. Not a peep! You won't even know I'm there."

"I can't."

"We watch everything together. Who are you going to hug when the Giants score?"

Dreams of glory, Christmas 1960.

"Hon, I'm sorry. There's no room in the car."

"Put me in the trunk. Wrap me in a blanket like a mob hit."

Dad lingered, then shook his head and continued to walk across the kitchen, his free leg doing all the work.

After he left, I fell apart. Rory understood and left me alone. Mom knew, too, and eased her rules. She let me loose in my room during the game.

I shared a bunk bed with Rory. Wisely, he avoided the space until the game was over. Mom gave me the kitchen radio but made me put it under the bunk bed, pushed way back. In the past, I had tripped over it, kicked it, and thrown it. Everything breakable was hidden. No one was allowed to throw a ball anywhere in the apartment since Dad had broken a window during a Yankee game.

Kickoff was a half hour away. With time to kill, I turned the radio to the pregame show and took out my lucky charms: old newspaper clippings of big Giant victories, Dad's game stubs with the score and weather written on each stub, and a commemorative coin from the 1956 championship season. It had all the opponents and scores for each game that year. During the game, I flipped it, talked to it, and kissed it for good luck before critical plays.

Once the game started, I began to run across the tops of the bunk bed, dresser, closet, and toy chest. Flying over the furniture, I made believe I was inside Yankee Stadium watching the game. I moved around the stands following the action. I sat in the box seats, the mezzanine, or the grandstand. I hailed a vendor for a Coke or a hotdog.

The mid-'60s Giants were terrible—a single victory was cause to schedule a parade. This game, against the Washington Redskins, was close; I grew nervous and quiet. Mom, curious when the racket died down, popped her head in.

"How they doing?" she said.

"Oh, we have the ball with under a minute to go and we're down by four points—we need good luck."

"Well, good luck," Mom said and started to leave.

"No, Mommo, we need good luck. You're my lucky charm. Please, let me put you in a headlock."

"No. You know I don't like anyone touching my head."

"Mom, just this once. The headlock will work. I feel it in my bones. Come on, do it for your Sonny Boy." I got down on one knee and spread my arms.

"I hate people near my head."

"Pretty please. It's the play of the game." I hit both knees. "One play and that's it."

Mom offered me her head and I gave her a gentle full Nelson, a classic wrestling move also used in roller derby matches. I imagined the fans sizing up the death match—a beautiful, dark-haired woman with circles under her eyes, wearing a flowery house dress with fluffy slippers, as her neck was wrung, sweetly, by her 10-year-old son. We held this position and listened to the radio.

Marty Glickman did the play by play. He usually took it harder than I did. "This is it," he said. "No matter what happens, this has been an amazing comeback by the much-maligned Giants this afternoon. Young Gary Wood, number 19, has replaced the injured Y. A. Tittle as quarterback. With under a minute to go, Giants have the ball, fourth down on the Redskins' one-yard line. It's their last chance."

Mom mumbled obscenities. I blocked them out, readjusted her head and directed my ear back to the announcer's voice: "Here we go. Wood leans over the center and takes the snap. He fakes a handoff to Webster, rolls left, lots of room— Wood's in the end zone standing up. Touchdown! The Giants lead, 12–10."

My arms swung up to signal the score. Taking advantage, Mom broke free from the headlock.

Glickman was shouting. "It's through there. The extra point is good. It's a high holy day for the faithful parishioners in the Church of Mara! The team chaplain, Father Benedict Dudley, is jumping up and down on the sidelines with his friend Wellington Mara, the Giants' owner. They're crushing each other's hats."

I soared. Father Dudley was the pastor of my church; I was one of his altar boys. I had an inside connection to the Giants' owner!

I reclaimed Mom's head, cuddled it and kissed it 13 times, one for each Giant point. She kept yelling: "Let me go! Let me go!"

"You are my lucky Uncle Mommy," I replied. "That's your new name, Uncle Mommy."

"I'm glad the Giants won," she said. "I like my new name. But you'll never get near my head again." Then she stumbled out of the room.

Forty-four years later, in 2008, I put my long-gone mother's favorite teddy bear in a headlock right before Lawrence Tynes, the Giants' place-kicker, lined up for an overtime field goal attempt in Green Bay. The kick was dead perfect. Giants 23, Packers 20.

Street Kid

1962–1967

Spotless Cleaners

Dad's pants vanish. All eyes are on me.

One night in 1964, as the Christmas break loomed, 13 inches of snow piled up on my street. When you're in fifth grade, losing a school day to the elements is a beautiful thing.

Friday morning, my friends and I mushed over to Central Park, towing our sleds through the middle of the street. Milking the day to the last of the light, we rode every hill until our feet froze. Back from sledding, I plopped down outside my apartment on the hall stairs and began undressing.

"King of the Hill," Rory, 83rd Street.

As usual, Mom had refused to let me inside the apartment. She, slush, and dog poop were mortal enemies. As I worked my top layer off, I heard my father's familiar step coming up the stairs.

He mumbled to himself, "Damn, I forgot the suit." Noticing me, his eyes focused on my half-untied snow boots. "Tommy here's the ticket, hurry to the cleaners. I need that suit for the wedding."

"OOOOOOOOOOhhhhhh," left my mouth as I dramatized the act of rising slowly. "Go!" Dad ordered.

I death-marched down the stairs. Dad behind me: "FASTER. They're going to close in five minutes."

When I got there, Joe, the manager of Spotless Cleaners, was turning off the lights. Smiling with an edge, he opened the door. "Come in, Tommy. Be quick. I want to get out of here."

Deed done. I had earned a slow walk home. A slow, meandering trek through every snow pile between the store and my building. Walking deliberately, I was Hannibal's elephant moving over the Alps, going knee-deep with every step. I created serpentine paths over each snow pile.

I moved the suit to the back of my peacoat, resting the hanger's hook on my collar. This left both hands free for better balance.

Reenacting the Punic Wars stretched my normal five-minute trip home to half an hour. With the satisfaction of a job well done, I danced a jig and rang the bell in the vestibule, signaling my return and also my incredible urge to pee. I ran up the stairs and Dad greeted me at the door. "Where the hell were you?"

I said nothing, smirked, and turned my back, offering Dad his suit from its resting place on the nape of my neck. In the hall I whipped my boots off and ran into the bathroom, working off my jeans, long johns, and two pairs of underwear just in time.

Dad met me face to face as I exited from the bathroom, holding up the suit.

"Nice jacket. Where are my pants?"

"Huh," I mumbled.

"My pants, where are my pants?"

A clothes hanger never had as thorough an examination as the one I put that hanger through. The pants were not on it, in it, on top of it or under it. There were no pants. The jacket, the jacket was good. Two sleeves, pressed, cleaned, all that. But the pants, the pants made no appearance despite multiple prayers under my breath. I was the baffled volunteer from the audience looking for the rabbit in the hat and finding unbelievably, it was gone!

Dad dressed and said, "Let's go."

Down to Hades we descended, third floor, second floor, first floor, no pants. Hallway, no pants. Down the building's front steps, no pants.

Dad said, "So which way did you walk exactly?"

This is where it got tricky. I set a new record for a dramatic pause. My mouth agape, he asked again, "Exactly— where—did—you—walk?"

Words failed me. I didn't even try. I had had too many fruitless experiences responding to similar questions from my father. They were unanswerable. So instead I showed him my exact path. Every nuance. Every turn. Every double step. The place where I did the cha-cha—one step up, two back, one up.

When Dad and I had these special moments an eerie stillness set in. No yelling, no accusations. Only the look punctuated with sharp orders: "Stop." "Go left." "Here?" "Are you sure you weren't under any cars?"

Hill after hill we climbed toward the avenue, policing the grounds. Despite the fact that Dad's pants were charcoal and the streets were blanketed in white snow, he insisted we walk very slowly.

When we got to the cleaners they were closed, and then we walked back to our building. Same story. After one last look under the car directly in front of the house, we entered the lobby and began our ascent—second floor, third floor, fourth floor—into the apartment. Passing through the door, Dad gave Mom the look and then me, one more look for good luck. He went directly to his jacket on the hanger with the plastic still on it. Dad held it up—then draped it over his arm. Together they resembled Michelangelo's Pietà. Dad was saying goodbye to the jacket and I swore I could hear that final conversation.

"We have closed many bars together, old friend," Dad sighed. "I will miss the way the secretary at Pepsi looked at you, on me, when we made our sales calls."

Dad said no more about the suit.

Two weeks later, I'm playing in front of the house and Dad comes walking up the street. Getting closer, I see he has on a charcoal jacket.

Oh God, I'm thinking, he bought the same suit again. Not good.

"Hi Dad, is that the suit? It looks great. Did you buy it again?"

"Nope, same one," Dad said with a smile. "Every suit comes with two pairs of pants."

Davy Jones' Locker

*At Joe's Candy Store, you have to plunge your arm
into the icy, numbing water of the cooler
to snag your favorite soda. Fail and it's jeers all around.*

The soda cooler in Joe's Candy Store was battered and colored red, with a raised Coca-Cola bottle cap on all four sides. A similar model followed Ike across Europe throughout World War II. I loved it. I kissed it when no one was looking.

The cooler was six feet long, three feet wide, and three feet deep. It rested on a wood base that lifted its height up by one foot. It sat in near darkness at the rear of the soda parlor. Upon close examination, you saw that it bled sweat and released a soft, steady hum.

Joe's was our neighborhood's home base and always crowded like a zoo. Until I knew better, I thought a bunch of kids lived there. Every day, Joe, a moody, 50-or-so-year-old bachelor, arrived at the store wearing grey work pants, a grey T-shirt, and a puss on his face. He was a man of few words. Here's a day's worth.

"What do you want?"

"Put the comic book back."

"In the right place."

"Get out."

Joe was a miser. He made Silas Marner look philanthropic. There were no fans in the store and minimal electricity. To save money he used low-wattage refrigerator and aquarium light bulbs in the space, giving it a glow of gloom.

Coming in from bright sunshine to a near-wartime blackout, you became disoriented. With enough kids in there you could get a good game of blind man's bluff going without the blindfold. Despite his record-breaking cheapness, Joe was no

Stanley Hom picking a winner.

fool. If you had a candy store you had to have ice-cold soda. Kids boycotted candy stores that ignored this rule.

The water temperature in Joe's cooler always flirted with the freezing mark. Sometimes, you needed to submarine your hand through a thin crust of ice forming on the surface. Two hundred bottles of soda, representing more than 20 different brands, were buried deep in that Arctic sea, in a light so dim the eels bumped into each other. With the cooler sitting on a foot-tall base, anyone less than four feet tall needed to lift himself to plunge into the Loch in search of Nessy.

I usually craved a bottle of Mission Cream. Unfortunately, Mission soda was a local brand and its many different flavors had zero variation in bottle style, texture or height. If you felt a Mission-shaped bottle deep in Joe's cooler, there was no way to know if it was orange or grape or cream or what.

All Missions being equal led me to give myself a pep talk before I attempted a plunge to find my favorite. "You can do it," I'd say. "I've seen you do it. Do it."

I'd hop up, and swing my arm over the cooler's front wall. My armpit was now responsible for keeping me airborne. I'd sink my other arm into the icy water with a numbing splash.

I was 100 percent dependent on my tactile skill for bottle retrieval. My hand and forearm would tighten up before I achieved bottle depth. When I reached it, my numb fingers would seek out and embrace the familiar Mission shape and pull it up.

"Ooooh," I would moan when I pulled up an orange or other unwanted flavor.

Back down the bottle would go. I'd do my best to remember where I replanted it. The bottles were snug as sardines. I had limited time before my arm below the elbow lost all sensation. Rotating my arm in a corkscrew motion increased blood circulation, allowing a brief search extension, but eventually the water was just too cold. Pride swallowed, I would raise the last bottle I touched before my hand passed out. If it was a root beer, grape or anything other than Mission Cream, I'd mutter, "Grrrrr."

I moved the not-ideal soda gently from my puffy blue hand to my other hand. I tucked my arm under my noncombatant armpit, rocking back and forth until warmth returned. With phony bravado, I grinned at my friends. A wicked pleasure swept through the crowd when someone chose a soda you knew wasn't their first choice. Everyone knew each other's favorite soda; that was right behind knowing their favorite sports team or movie star. When I was in the hot seat, I sat there drinking the soda, faking enjoyment, saying "Mmmm" or "Aaahhh," followed by a satisfied swipe of my mouth. I knew, they knew, I was lying. It didn't matter. I went down swinging.

"I do like it, I really do like it," I'd say. "I just didn't tell anybody."

One day, when I was eight, I was moping around the store. Joe, ready to throw me out, switched moods and asked me to take a newspaper around the corner to Mrs. Todero. I did. Two weeks later, Mrs. Moose was added to my delivery route. After a month, Joe asked me if I wanted to deliver *The New York Times* on Sunday mornings. He said my pay would be a dollar and any flavor milk shake I wanted. Excellent money. I knew I'd get decent tips so the dollar pay was gravy. On the first Sunday I showed up at 7 a.m. Joe gave me fifteen papers to pile into a grocery-shopping cart he told me was on loan from Sloan's Supermarket. "On loan?" I thought. "That's nice." Two hours later, three dollars richer in tips, I returned to the store triumphantly, with an empty cart and an awful milk shake craving.

"I'm back."

Behind the counter, Joe gave me a grunt with not much mood. I rode the cart to the back of the store and returned to the counter for my beautiful reward. I was in a death-match struggle between chocolate and vanilla, vanilla and chocolate. They were both so good and I didn't want to wait until next week for either one. Mom did this black and white thing with her egg creams and I toyed with that idea for a while, but I finally settled on chocolate.

"Joe, I'm ready."

"What flavor do you want?"

"I'd love a chocolate shake, please."

My tongue circled my lips. I spun around on the counter stool to see how many I could do. My record was five. I eased my effort, not wanting to be too dizzy while sucking down the shake. Soon the rumble of the mixer died down. I turned as Joe approached me with a big smile. This unnerved me. It took a while to leave his smile and redirect my eyes to the important matter, my delicious chocolate shake. I looked down. I smelled it before I fully thought out the word...strawberry...strawberry?.... Joe walked away before I could confront him. I began to present my case toward his back.

"Joe, I asked for chocolate. This is not chocolate. I don't like strawberry. I can't eat it."

Joe never turned around. I didn't see his face the whole time I sat there playing with the shake. After it got lukewarm, I pushed it to the edge of the counter. On the way out, I said goodbye. Joe was washing the long stirring spoons—for the second time in ten minutes.

"Hey Joe, can I get a chocolate shake next week?"

"Yeah."

"Promise?"

"Yep."

Liar, I thought.

Joe never made me a chocolate, vanilla, or black and white shake. I stopped hopping on the counter after Sunday paper deliveries. What was the point? Joe delivered a strawberry shake each time. At least he stopped smiling. Over time, I realized that Mr. Stingy was moving his stock and the strawberry had to go. My compensation sank back to a dollar. I hardly noticed. At eight years old, counting tips, four dollars in my pocket made me a wealthy man.

You Say Tomato, I Say...

In preparing a tuna sandwich,
add the Hellman's last, Dad advises. Mom begs to differ.

"That's not how you do it."

Dad grabbed the yellow mixing bowl from Mom.

"Oh really, Mr. Wizard?"

"You don't stab the tuna; you press the fork down into the tuna like a pharmacist crushes tablets using a mortar and pestle. Grinding it, that's how it blends best with the mayo. And, you add the Hellman's last!"

Mom ripped the bowl back from Dad and said, "Take a hike."

Rory scratched his crew cut. It was fall 1962; he and I were six and eight years old, and we had no idea what a pestle or a mortar was. We only wanted a tuna sandwich and this argument was a repeat.

After Mom stingily spread the tuna on Wonder bread, making three sandwiches from one can, she began to cut them in halves. Dad came back.

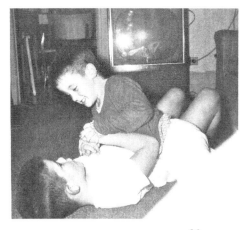

Brother pins brother.

"Cut them on the bias."

"Huh?" Rory and I exchanged puzzled looks as another word we didn't understand interfered with our lunch.

"What?" Mom's eyes went wide.

"If you cut them on the bias, the sandwich tastes better. It's all about the presentation."

Dad cut one sandwich.

"You're a hot air balloon, blow away." Mom pushed him out of the kitchen.

Rory and I measured the sandwiches' size with our eyes and each reached for the fattest one. Mom got it first.

After we devoured the sandwiches, Rory and I battled over who would clean the bowl with an extra piece of bread. During the pulling portion, the thick glass bowl dropped to the linoleum floor and rolled to the stove. Rory and I dove for it. Mom separated us by our necks and threw us into the hallway.

Down four flights into the street—Rory went one way, and I went the other.

I headed down to the hockey field at Carl Schurz Park. There were some guys playing touch football, fathers playing basketball, and several young mothers with strollers. Bored, waiting to play something, I put Joe Menesick into a headlock and we started wrestling. He pinned me. Out of nowhere Rory flew in thinking it was a real fight, and punched Joe in the head.

Joe yelled "Oow!" and slugged Rory. I hit Joe. Dennis, Joe's brother, who had been playing football, saw this and jumped in, thinking Joe was in trouble. Now it was a two on two, full-blown, double-brother fight. All the kids circled the scrum, watching. After a while, two fathers playing basketball came over and broke it up. One father didn't like the way the other father looked at him, and said so. That fellow hit the other dad and the two of them started fighting. Rory, Joe, Dennis, and I dropped away from the crowd and strolled out of the park laughing. Rory and I walked home together, not saying anything.

It was 5:30 when we got home. My parents announced that they were going to the RKO to see *The Manchurian Candidate*, and that we were going to my dad's parents' house for dinner. This was good. Large Nan and large Pop loved food. We called their refrigerator "Treasure Island."

Pop met us at the door and gave us bear hugs. "No Nonsense" Nan was sitting in her chair, crocheting a blanket for a friend. She said "Hi" to us and then, to Pop, "Johnny, I need more blue and green wool. Get the car."

"Noooo," I thought, "late dinner." Pop got the '52 Plymouth and we headed down the FDR to Grand Street, the wool source. Pop parked in front of the store with the colorful striped awning, and Nan left her large tote bag in the car, so she could swindle a couple of those heavy-duty, white, Grand Street shopping bags from the store clerk. Sturdy bags were essential to collect field supplies.

While Nan shopped, Rory and I fought, first arguing over where we'd go on vacation next year, Disneyland or Niagara Falls. We never went anywhere on vacation, other than a day trip to Rockaway Beach. Then the imaginary vacation squabble turned into a thigh-pinching contest—which led to open warfare.

We wrestled ourselves from the back seat up into the car's rear window area. We crushed the cardboard Kleenex box and knocked the head off the bobblehead boxer dog with the brown felt pelt that sat in the center of the rear window. Pop loved that dog.

That was the only time I remember Pop getting seriously mad at us. He came over the front seat and extended his grizzly-sized body toward us, with his big belly flopping in the air over the back seats until his angry face met our faces—didn't touch us, didn't scream, but the whites of his eyes gave Rory and me reason to employ our rarely used good-grandson-waiting pose.

Settled back in my seat, looking at the back of Pop's head, I thought of the witch in *Snow White*. Pop's head was the same bright-red color as her poisoned apple.

Then a pretty lady with a white cap came over and leaned into Pop's window. "Mister, you OK? You don't look good."

She took his hand in hers. "I'm a nurse, sir, and based on the pulse I'm feeling, you're going to have a heart attack if you don't calm down."

Around this time, Nan came out of the store and saw an attractive, leggy, curly-haired blond talking low and sweet to Pop while she stroked his hand.

Nan put half of her body through the open passenger side window and said, "Anything interesting?"

"Ma'am, everything's fine, I just thought this gentleman looked distressed," said the beautiful lady.

"Let's find out and ask my HUSBAND. Johnny, are you distressed?"

Pop said nothing.

"Sorry ma'am, I didn't intend to cause any trouble. I was just here in the street, taking people's blood pressure and I happened to see…"

"…my husband." Nan cut her off.

"Yes, your husband—looking poorly. Well, he seems to be doing much better now, so I'll leave you be."

"Bye!" Nan said, while kicking Pop in the leg.

When we drove away there was silence, until Pop turned north up First Avenue. Then, Nan threw out the question, "What the hell was that about?"

Pop slowed the car, looked back at us, then turned to Nan and let it fly. "Did you order us down here? Did you get what you wanted? Were you in the car when the lady approached me with our kids in the car? No, so you have no idea why that lady came to my window. All you have are your presumptions, which are always right. So, for the first time ever, I'm telling you nothing. Think what you want, the world doesn't revolve around you."

Nan's mouth stayed open for the entire ride. Pop went silent until a Checker cab cut him off when we exited the U.N. tunnel at 49th Street, and then he let Nan have it a second time. We didn't make a peep. Our mouths were open as wide as Nan's. They dropped us off in front of our house on 83rd Street without a good-bye. As soon as they pulled away, I heard Pop's voice rising.

When we walked into our apartment, Dad was in the kitchen drawing a group of trees and Mom was lounging on the couch in the living room watching *The World at War.*

"How are you guys?" Dad asked.

"Fine," I said as we disappeared into our bedroom.

"We didn't eat," Rory said.

I smacked my head.

"What do you mean you didn't eat? Nan and Pop didn't feed you?"

"No," Rory said.

"Here it comes," I thought. "We're dead." I was worried we'd get blamed for their fight.

"Why?" Dad asked Rory.

"They forgot."

"Why'd they forget?"

Dad's sketch.

"They were fighting."

"What?"

I peeked into the kitchen from our bedroom doorway. Dad looked shocked.

Mom walked into the kitchen from the living room, stroked Rory's hair, put him on her lap, and said softly, "Honey, tell me the whole story."

Rory took a deep breath. "Nan needed wool, so we went to the store downtown. A lady talked to Pop. Nan talked to the lady. We drove away. A little later, Nan asked Pop or maybe all of us a question, then Pop yelled at Nan for asking the question. Then Pop stopped yelling. Later, a car cut him off, and Pop remembered he was still mad at Nan, and he started yelling at her again. Then they dropped us off and forgot to feed us. When they drove away I heard Pop yell one more time."

During Rory's speech, I walked into the kitchen. When Rory was done, Mom started laughing and Dad looked like he couldn't decide what face to put on. Finally, he slipped into a grin and started to laugh low, then harder, just as loud as Mom. Mom stood and leaned on Dad's shoulder for support and the both of them laughed so hard, I saw their stomachs going in and out in rhythm. That was a new picture. I went to the refrigerator, grabbed three slices of Swiss cheese, gave Rory two, and a love tap on his head.

Perfect Day

No adult lecture can dampen my mood. I am invincible.
It is June 21, 1964, fourth grade is a distant memory,
and the summer stretches endlessly, gloriously ahead.

"Do you wait until you're done?"

"Yes," I said as I stepped out of our bathroom.

"I mean, do you wait until you're sure you're finished?" Mom asked.

"I really do."

"Obviously, you don't," Mom said, wagging a finger at the stream of pee meandering down my left pant leg.

"It fools me."

"Well, why don't you fool it back? Make believe you're putting it away, then leave it out and see what happens?"

"For how long?"

"Get your shoes on, get your brother, and let's go," Mom said, losing steam. "If we're lucky, we'll sneak in before the Gospel."

No adult lecture could dampen my mood. I was invincible. It was the 1964 summer solstice—June 21st, sunset at 8:31 p.m.—confirmed by consultation with my *Reader's Digest Farmers Almanac* calendar. I had been liberated from fourth grade two days before, and now I faced the first of an endless string of Sundays free of the looming gloom of Monday. On Sunday, during the school year, I would always carry a nagging dread of the next day through all of my activities. Summer empowers Sunday!

Nine o'clock Mass was always a sellout. Avoiding the browbeating ushers, we tried slipping into a pew crowded shoulder to shoulder in the back of the church. Rory led, I followed, then Mom. Mom pushed me, I pushed Rory, and Rory pushed a holy-roller lady and she said, "Well, I never!"

On the altar, Father Edward O'Holleran stopped his prayer, dropped his raised arms to his side, turned his head slowly, and glared at Mom. I flipped my head towards Rory and silently mouthed the words, "What are you gonna do?"

"Thanks a lot," Mom mouthed back.

After Mass, I ran home to put on my sneakers, shorts, and T-shirt. It was ten o'clock; there were only eleven hours left of daylight and so much to do. First, I had to finish Dad's Father's Day card. I had time. Around two o'clock the night before, Dad fumbled with his keys in the hallway, came in and banged around. After a short banging break, he put on his bedroom light and yelled at Mom, "There's nothing to eat!" He made a racket until he found two cans of sardines and a box of Saltine crackers. After he ate, he turned on the TV but Mom got up and shoved him into bed. This morning Dad was sleeping in.

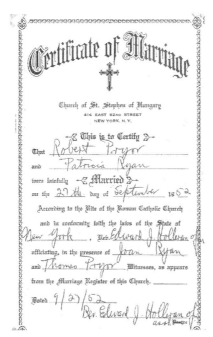

Mom and Dad make it legal with Father Edward in 1952.

I cut a Joe DiMaggio photo out of *Life Magazine* taken in the Yankee Clipper's rookie year, 1937. Joe, with his gap-toothed smile, had his bat slung lazily over his shoulder. From the same magazine, I tore out a photo of a young Frank Sinatra in a zoot suit singing to a bunch of squealing girls in the Paramount Theater. I placed Dad's two favorite guys next to each other on the front of the card and pasted dialogue bubbles over their heads.

DiMaggio said, "Dear Bob, your Sonny Boy said you're the *Best Dad in the World*, so I'm going to go five-for-five today and smack two homers into the left field bleachers just for you. Happy Father's Day, Love, Joltin' Joe."

Sinatra said, "Hey Bobby, your son Tommy thinks you're his *Night and Day*. Happy Pappy's Day! Ring-a-Ding-Ding! Love, Francis Albert."

I wrote Dad a poem inside the card. It was kind of personal, just between him and me. When I finished, I went to his bedroom and gently left it on Mom's pillow next to his sleeping head.

Job done, I flew down the hall stairs. Surveying the scene from my stoop, I saw circles of kids and had several options. The hot sun baked the stoop railing. I needed fuel.

My first stop, Joe's Candy Store, was lit by his usual two chintzy light bulbs. He pulled the window shades down to cool the space. His ceiling fan coughed and shook but delivered no breeze.

"Hi, Joe," I said.

He grunted at me.

This was progress. He usually ignored customers unless they were paying for something or he was throwing them out. I looked through the sports magazines and comics for new stuff. Nothing.

"Hey Joe, were there any deliveries this week?"

"No."

"Bye, Joe," I said, just to get my goodbye grunt.

Two stores down was Parker's Grocery. Year-round, Murray Parker wore a girl-catching Elmer Fudd leather hunting hat, with earflaps, on his shiny bald head. His giant black-rimmed eyeglasses were the ideal accessory.

When I was desperate for a Mission cream soda I could make a sure pick at Parker's, where I could see what I was doing. Unlike at Joe's, shopping didn't require a flashlight.

That day Murray was helping a customer, Mrs. Hutznagel, a gigantic pain in the ass. All the storeowners called her "Sourpuss." She was buying cheese and cold cuts and Murray was at the slicer. I watched from the back of the store while weighing my soda selection. I saw sweat rolling down his chipmunk cheeks.

"Murray, make sure the cheese is paper thin," she barked three times.

Murray delicately raised two fingers "holding" a slice of air and asked, "Is this thin enough?"

Sourpuss ignored him and played with the fruit. She squeezed every piece, and then threw it back. I saw Murray mumbling. He needed cheering up.

Murray had a long counter that ran the length of the store. I stood on Murray's side of the counter so Mrs. Hutznagel couldn't see me, but Murray could. Every pair of shorts I owned had a worn hole somewhere around the crotch area. I found the hole in my current pair and carefully pulled out part of my ball sac (without a ball), giving it fresh air. I waited until Murray shut off the slicer.

"Hey, Murray," I said. "You want to see me blow up my balloon?"

When I had his full attention, I squeezed one of my nuts through the hole into my deflated sac, making it swell up like one of Dizzy Gillespie's cheeks. Murray started choking. He stepped back so he could lean against the cash register and try to recover. Each time he thought he was OK he'd look back at me. When he did, I'd do it again. His hat and glasses were crooked and he began to cry and laugh at the same time. I was so proud.

"Murray, are you OK? Are you OK?" Mrs. Hutznagel thought he was having a fit. It was time to leave. I left 12 cents on the counter for the Mission cream and waved 'bye.

Back on my block there were several games in progress. I worked my way down the street and joined the ones that moved me. First, I played a little "Ace, King, Queen," then I jumped into "Off the Point"—two games played with a Spaldeen (a pink reject tennis ball tattooed with the name, "Spalding.")

Spaldeens were serious business. I tested their quality by dropping them from shoulder height. The higher the bounce, the better the ball. Joe had lots of Spaldeens, and they sat in a tall wire barrel near the cash register. Kids were always trying to sneak a ball in their pocket, so Joe kept a close eye on the bin. During the quality tests I conducted at the bin, I developed immunity to being shooed and Joe became a genuine conversationalist.

"Pick a ball and get out of here."

"That's what I'm trying to do."

"They're all good." He grabbed one and squeezed it. "See?"

"Yes," I said. "But one of them is better than all the others."

He studied me. "You just tried that one," he said.

"Not true. I have a system. I repeat no ball."

"I repeat: Pick a friggin' ball—Now!"

I'd find a ball, say " 'Bye, Joe," and leave a quarter on the counter.

Around noon, the dads started popping up. Normally, most dads would head straight for the bars on a hot Sunday afternoon, but since it was Father's Day that wouldn't be right. They stood on top of the stoops, surveying the block. The older boys were playing stickball. A few mothers had their front windows wide open, looking for a breeze. I heard Dean Martin's voice floating in the air crooning, "Everybody Loves Somebody." Looking up, I saw Mrs. Palermo draped over her windowsill, singing along with Dino and bopping her blond hair in time with the song. The dads congregated around the older boys' home plate—a manhole cover at the eastern end of the street.

"You play like girls," one dad said.

"We could beat you in our sleep," said another father.

"Prove it, old man," a teenager said, adding, "Put up or shut up."

That insult ended the debate—there'd be a game. Dad remained on our stoop, amusing himself by listening to the banter. He yelled down to the group, "Let's make it interesting. The dads take the little guys on our team."

The teenagers sneered, but the young guys got into the game. I never played in a competitive game alongside Dad; we'd just play catch and pitch to each other. I couldn't stop grinning.

Stickball wasn't easy. The bat was a broomstick. The field included the sidewalk, cars, building walls, trees, and fire escapes. Everything was in play. It was a bona fide talent to be able to follow a bouncing ball down a web of fire escape landings and windowsills and catch the wobbly egg in your cupped hands. The ball was small and light and you needed to finesse its capture. In the street game of stickball we pitched it into the batter on one bounce. Stickball was also played against a wall on the sidewalk. You fast-pitched the Spaldeen from an imaginary mound in the street toward a strike zone we had chalked on a building's wall where the batter stood ready in his stance.

Paddy McNamara's father, a lieutenant in the Yorkville police precinct, just happened to have a parade sawhorse in the basement of his building that he dragged out for special occasions. To start the game, Mr. Mac plopped the sawhorse at the end of 83rd Street where it met East End Avenue, shutting off car traffic for the rest of the day. Walking back toward the group, Mr. Mac tipped his cap to acknowledge the round of applause from the audience. His smooth style reminded me of Jimmy Cagney in *Yankee Doodle Dandy*.

My Uncle Mickey, and my dad's friend Allie, were on our team, both good players and unusual characters. On one play, Allie dove into a row of garbage cans to catch a line drive. All the cans rolled over, the garbage flew out and Allie came up holding the ball.

Mickey went over, examined Allie's wrist, held Allie's arm straight up and said, "Takes a licking and keeps on ticking!"

"I'm not a watch, Doc," Allie smirked, letting Mickey know he got the reference to the Timex television commercial. Then he threw the ball back to me.

Later in the game, Mickey waited for a ball to make its way down a whole building's-worth of fire escapes.

Staring up, he said, "Round and round it goes, where it stops nobody knows."

After one last, weird bounce, the ball eased into Mickey's hands.

During the fifth inning, someone yelled, "Hey, look!" and pointed up toward a building. There was a guy in a T-shirt running up a fire escape with a portable TV under his arm. It was our neighborhood junkie, Freddie Hammer. Chasing him was Mr. Fletcher, who must've come home while Freddie was helping himself to the TV. Freddie had the lead, but looked like he was getting winded. I didn't like Mr. Fletcher and was pulling for Freddie.

"Come on Freddie, you can do it! Get to the roof, get to the roof."

With Freddie in the lead he, the TV, and Mr. Fletcher disappeared over the roof and we went back to the game.

We played three games. We won the first one. The teenagers won the second one. Then we played the rubber match. Dad got two hits in the third game and pitched great. We won 3–2. The teens begged for a best of five, but the dads told them to take a hike.

The heat was brutal and we were sweaty and exhausted. Mr. Mac went down to his basement again and came back with a giant wrench. He had a large tool collection from his days as a beat cop, when he confiscated wrenches from kids who illegally turned on "Johnny pumps."

Mr. Mac went to the fire hydrant and flooded the street. Steam rose off the scorched asphalt and the air filled with a cooling mist. My skin goose-bumped. The rush of the water drowned out all other sound. I protected my transistor radio, putting it to my ear to get the baseball scores. I normally listened to the Yankee game, but a Phillies pitcher, Jim Bunning, had retired 15 Mets in a row. He was perfect through five. I yelled, "The Mets are being no-hitted!"

Then Rory held my radio while I dove headfirst onto the water gushing out of the hydrant. It exploded out syrup-thick, giving me an opportunity to ride a cushioned wave if I hit it perfect. On the other hand, if I missed the wave, hello asphalt. In the past, this has led to torn clothing, cuts, and once, a visit to the emergency room at Lenox Hill Hospital. This day, my dive was half-assed. The East German judge gave me a five.

It slipped my mind that Dad was watching the action. He never approved of hydrant play, and he never joined in when we engaged in it. Dad expected perfect behavior, and frowned on less. This day was different. Thanks to Lieutenant McNamara, it was an inside job.

Rory passed the radio back to me, screamed "Gangway!" and leaped into the air for a beautiful ride. Rory was a graceful and fearless eight-year-old. I went back to the game and heard the Mets announcer, Lindsey Nelson, say, "At the end of seven, it's the Phillies six and the Mets nothing. Bunning's retired 21 straight batters."

"He's perfect through seven," I said.

By this time, even Met fans were into it and there were so many radios turned on that the sound of the game was beginning to match the roar of the hydrant. I turned toward the pump and saw Dad directing the water. He was squatting behind the hydrant in a catcher's position, reaching his long arms around the fireplug and giving it a big hug. With his fists together, he came up under the jet of water and began to lift the spray skyward, as if it was a fireboat in the East River. Higher and higher he sent it, up to a second-story fire escape across the street. His eyes opened wide and he laughed hard. Dad kept the arc of water up there for a few minutes until he realized he'd knocked over Mrs. Trusits' flowerpots. I watched his face. It said, "Uh-oh." He was ten again. When he brought the water spray back to ground level, I left the bag and stole second base.

"Nice slide, Tommy," I heard Dad say over the noise.

As word got around that the Mets were down to their last batter in the ninth, Dad turned the hydrant off. He was soaked, his T-shirt dripping.

All ears tilted toward the voice on the radio.

"Hello everybody, what a day for Bunning, two hits and two RBIs on top of retiring 26 straight Mets in this 91-degree heat. To the plate steps pinch-hitter John Stephenson. Mets are down to their last out. 32,000 fans are on their feet. Here's the pitch. A called first strike. The crowd's clapping as Bunning rubs the ball. The windup... he delivers... Strike two! Bunning circles the mound and returns to the rubber. The catcher gives him the signal. Bunning draws a big breath, the windup, and the pitch... Stephenson swings... Strike three! He did it! He did it! A perfect game! The Phillies are mobbing Bunning, slapping him, hugging him, throwing him up on their shoulders. On only 90 pitches, Bunning makes history."

The Yankee fans went bananas; the Mets fans sulked. This lasted a few minutes, and then Dad turned the hydrant back on. An hour later, I don't know who brought it up first, but no one had eaten all day. It was near six o'clock and it seemed everyone's stomach woke up at the same time.

Chickie Murphy, watching from her fourth floor window, overheard the food reference. "I ain't friggin' cooking, so here's a bag of sandwiches for my kids and knucklehead husband. Here, catch."

Pretty Chickie threw a bag out the window. It came down like a rock and missed her son's head by inches. He picked it up and took out sandwiches in wax paper, then another mother did the same thing, and before long everybody had something in their mouth—Kaiser roll, banana, Yankee Doodle, Ring Ding, anything to keep us going. And that was that. By the time we finished eating and farting around it was well past 8 o'clock and the sun was sinking behind the Metropolitan Museum of Art on Fifth Avenue. A group of kids sat on the stoop singing along with Peter and Gordon to "World Without Love," on the radio. The girls loved the song. The boys teased them by covering their hearts.

When the streetlights came on, everyone was still milling around. The light over our stoop was broke. Who cared?

"Let's take this party to the Old Timers," a voice came out of the twilight. Everyone whooped it up like a posse in an old Western and the crowd moved as one around the corner. The Old Timers Tavern sat in the storefront next to Nan Rode's house. I ran into the bar, dropped a dime in the jukebox and played a fast one with lots of thumping; "You Can't Sit Down," by The Dovels.

Everyone passing through the tavern's door shook something in time to the music. Some their hips, others their leg, some just put a finger in the air and wagged it back and forth. The regulars on the barstools thought we were all nuts and kept drinking their short beers. The place had a great dance floor in the back. All the kids and many of the mothers headed there and the dads joined the regulars at the bar. Us kids took over the long polished shuffleboard game and rotated between playing that game and making whirling dizzying spins on the dance floor when a song moved us.

Eventually, not without a fight, Rory gave in and fell asleep across two chairs. A chocolate candy bar dangled from his mouth. Dad removed the Milky Way and carried Rory over his shoulder up the stairs to Nan Rode's second-floor apartment. By the time Dad came back, I was punchy, lying on the floor watching the fan's rotation. Dad picked me up, nuzzled my head with his chin and put me over his shoulder. I smelled his short dark hair and leaned into the nape of his

"Kilroy was here!" Thirsty gents posing inside The Old Timers Tavern.
Dad is guy with butt and short beer.

strong neck. He carried me upstairs, and laid me down next to Rory in the bed.

"How about that Bunning, Dad?"

"Perfect, Tommy. Thanks for the card, Hon."

"Happy Father's Day," I said, straining to keep my eyes open.

He smiled and kissed my forehead. I smiled back, thinking, "There'll be no arguing or yelling tonight."

Free Skirt Steak

Nan Rode teaches me the principles of smart meat shopping, including the beauty of the paper-thin cutlet.

"Tommy, get my bag," my grandmother barked. It was February 1965. I was 11.

"Oh, Christ," I thought. Slowly, I made my way through the railroad flat looking for Nan Rode's pocketbook. It weighed more than my little brother, and when I heaved the thing up, I imagined Nan in the audience on *Let's Make A Deal*, easily meeting Monty Hall's challenge to draw an Indian head penny out of the bag, or a 1928 Al Smith for President pencil with Al's head and big nose on the top (I still have that item).

I muscled the bag into the kitchen. Nan wanted to give me money because it was Saturday, and Saturday meant I was going shopping.

Nan liked Schaller & Weber's frankfurters, Karl Ehmer's pork chops and bologna, and Reliable Meats' veal cutlets. Plus, George at Reliable Meats on York Avenue would throw in a half-pound of skirt steak if he was in a good mood.

Schaller & Weber was my first stop, and there was always a major crowd there on Saturdays. I wanted to play ball sometime that day, so I'd minimize my wait by getting there early. Nan had specific shopping directions for each location.

Schaller & Weber: "Make sure you see the guy's hands at all times. If they drop below the counter, and he comes up with franks, tell him to put them back, and take the fresh ones out of the glass display."

I watched the guy's hands like he was a card cheat. And there he went—"Hey Mister, I don't want those franks, give me two pounds of these." I pointed to the glass. The guy gave me a dirty look and put the old franks back below the counter.

Next stop was Karl Ehmer's. I reviewed Nan's instructions for that store: "Tell the guy to leave all the fat on the pork chops."

The Karl Ehmer butcher loved me. I'd point out pork chops in the glass and he'd grab them and wrap them in paper. He never even had to pick up a trim knife.

After Ehmer's, I walked down 85th Street with five pounds of meat in paper bags. All the dogs I passed on the sidewalk looked at me funny and moaned.

Halfway down the block, Nan's final directions pop into my head: "Make sure George pounds the cutlets paper thin and throws in the skirt steak. Don't forget the steak!"

George was a problem. He knew my large grandmother bought lots of meat, but bought only part of her meat from him. He wanted all of her business. There was no way I'd bring the other meat into his store—he'd torture me—but I was too lazy to run it up to my grandmother's apartment one building away. So, I'd hide it outside the shop—in the gutter hugging the curb, in the basket of the delivery bike, or throw it onto an awning. I had plenty of places to put it but they all had potential consequences. Lots of kids and animals comb the gutter for goodies, and they might pick it up and eat a frank right there. The delivery boy could slip by me and take my meat for an unwanted ride. Up on the awning, pigeons could use the bags for target practice, or I might not be able to find something to reach the bags to get them down.

"Why you so antsy?" George asked.

"Huh?"

"What are you looking for?"

"Nothing."

I was second on line, and George was working alone. He was annoyed that I kept asking the lady behind me with the baby to hold my place, while I checked on my hidden stash.

When it was my turn, George leaned over the counter. I could smell his coffee and cigarette breath.

"No franks and chops today?"

He knew. He knew everyone's meat desires.

Murray Parker, apparently recovered from my visit, was one of the grocers Nan kept in line.

"No thank you, George, just the cutlets. Please give them a good pounding. Nan says, 'nice and lean!' "

He hit the meat like it was my head. Then he put my stuff in a bag and eyed me over. I gave him a nod toward the skirt steak with a pathetic look. He grudgingly wrapped a chunk in paper and threw it in the bag.

On the way out, George shouted a farewell.

"How long was the line at Schaller & Weber's?"

The hair on my neck stood up, but I didn't turn around. I looked for something to knock my bags off the Chinese laundry's awning.

I Love Catch

Steve Murphy and I play catch for 12 hours straight—even while cooking grilled cheese sandwiches in Nan's kitchen.

I love catch. Growing up, I always carried a football. It didn't matter what time of year it was, I carried one. You never knew when someone would want to play catch with you. You can't play catch without a ball. I stood ready.

I'd lie on my bed twirling the ball over my head, endlessly pursuing the perfect spiral. I rolled my fingers over the raised leather grain. Each throw was farther behind my head so I had to reach back and stretch.

I can hear the sound of a football as I release it near my ear, a soft "Whoosh!" If a hard-thrown ball came my way I'd ease the tension in my hands and hold them just right—like catching an egg. I could play catch for 12 hours straight and *did* play catch for 12 hours straight, with Steve Murphy, on Aug. 29, 1966. We kept the ball going through a grilled Swiss cheese sandwich in my grandmother's apartment sometime in the middle of the event. She never asked why we kept throwing the ball while we cooked and ate. We memorialized the event by penning the date on the ball.

My catch mentor, Dad, used to throw pillows around the living room. Mom learned to move lamps and vases before a game. If she left the house before a sporting event, she always said to Dad, "Don't throw anything, including the kids." Mom tried to hide the pillows but Dad always found them. After there was a good play on TV, his throw was accurate and the pillow landed safely on the seat of a chair or on the couch, or, best, in my arms. After a bad play, I ducked. Once, Mickey Mantle struck out with the bases loaded in the ninth inning against the Washington Senators. "The lousy last-place Senators, can you believe it?" he yelled at no one. As his sidekick, I felt his pain. Dad's face would turn beet red and strange words would come out of his mouth. They started off as curse words but got mangled and then bumped into each other.

Throughout Mantle's doomed at-bat against the Senators, Dad paced the room. I shadowed his moves two feet behind him. Rory in his playpen was a non-combatant. On every pitch, Dad halted, then held his breath. After the ball smacked into the catcher's mitt and the Yankee announcer moaned, "Strike three," the pillow he was squeezing the life out of flew through the air. It breezed over my ducking head and sailed through the open window. I watched its flight. It passed our fire escape, traveling about ten feet beyond the window. It hung in the air for a moment and then dropped into our neighbor's backyard, four flights below.

Dad sighed as it disappeared from view. Luckily, Mom wasn't home. Dad told me to keep an eye on Rory, who was playing with a yellow dump truck. He took the stairs to the first floor, climbed through Mrs. Hauser's kitchen window, went into the backyard, and retrieved the pillow. Rory and I watched the rescue from above. Dad pulled himself back up through Mrs. Hauser's window with one arm. Rory and I nodded to each other. Dad was a great tree climber. His practice was paying off.

* * *

Around the corner on the ground floor of Nan Rode's York Avenue building were two storefronts. To the left was Murray Parker's grocery, where, one day in 1963, I noticed a quart of milk, a loaf of Wonder Bread, and a pound of Ronzoni No. 9 spaghetti each cost 19 cents. This fact gave me joy.

To the right was Spotless Cleaners. Its sole employee, Joe, was my other catch mentor. Spotless was a franchise operation. You dropped your clothes off, they sent them to a factory where the work was done, and the clothes were returned the next day. For that reason Spotless was indeed spotless—clean white floors, clean white walls, no odors, no

Big game, Carl Schurz Park, 1961.

equipment—only the returned, cleaned clothes in neat rows on hangers, all in plastic wrapping.

Due to mid-day business being slow, Joe had lots of time to play catch with me. He was an athletic twenty-something with gifted hands. He resembled Elston Howard, the New York Yankee catcher. I'd throw the ball high, where no one but Joe could reach it. He was easily capable of throwing a football beyond two sewers, a benchmark of extraordinary talent that made him a neighborhood god. No matter how far or fast I ran, Joe always threw the ball far enough for me to run under it, rather than come back to meet the ball. This is an important catch fact. In catch, coming back for a ball is a cruel disappointment; it's always more satisfying to trap it on the fly.

Joe and I played catch for hours every week. During red lights we'd move our game from the sidewalk to the middle of York Avenue and Joe would throw long, high passes to me while I was running out at full speed. I'd snare the ball while making sure to avoid the idling cars at the corner waiting for the green light.

One day I puttered around the front of the store, waiting for Joe who was helping a few people with their clothes balled up in their arms. "Let's go Joe, let's go Joe," I said low, while petting a customer's cocker spaniel.

To calm my nerves, I played with the automatic shoeshine machine—the kind with thick rotating brushes around ankle level—one brush was black for dark shoes and one was tan for brown shoes. The "start" button was at the top. There was a small sign above the start button picturing a smiling man in a sharp suit saying, "Please Clean Your Shoes, Compliments of Spotless Cleaners!"

"Ah, an invitation!" I thought. "Well there you go! Let me polish my dirty sneakers…." I hadn't noticed that my sneakers were smeared with dog poop. When the rotating brush hit my sneaker, the poop flew free, whacking the clean white wall like brain matter exiting a head wound. It all happened for me in slow motion, frame by frame. Not all the poop hit the wall. Chunks landed on the dog owner customer and her cocker spaniel. I'm not sure how much time passed during the event—but I do remember having several thoughts about how this was going to lead to my death. I ran from the store like a rummy bolting a liquor store with a stolen pint bottle under his flapping coat. I was one step ahead of Joe, his arms greedily reaching out for me.

I ran up York Avenue toward 84th Street, where I passed my grandmother. She was carrying packages and I managed to greet her with a "Hi, Nan!" I caught a fleeting glance of her swiveling neck and open mouth as she pivoted to watch the tall angry man chasing me. Later that evening, I called

Nan to tell her what happened. She made no comment. Not a word. Ever.

Over the next few weeks, I walked to my grandmother's the long way—down 83rd Street, up East End Avenue, up 84th Street to York Avenue—to avoid Joe inside Spotless. Two weeks later, I stepped out of my grandmother's hall, turned north, and heard a voice over my shoulder, "Tommy, you wanna play catch?" It was Joe.

I love catch.

Nan's Two Birthdays

A lazy midwife was the reason for my grandmother's special circumstance. Nan proudly admits it turned her into a spoiled brat.

My grandmother Nan Rode's four-room railroad flat faced York Avenue in the front and a backyard in the rear. Leaning out her front window, I could watch my then world pass by. Leaning out her rear window, I could see Yorkville as it was a long time before even World War I. In the backyard was an old two-story house surrounded by five-story brick tenements.

The house, built around 1895, looked like it had fallen out of the sky and plopped onto a stray witch. Somehow, it had escaped the tenement explosion during the first two decades of the 1900s, a frenzy triggered by speculation about the underground IRT subway that would come to 86th Street and then proceed farther north. (This speculation ultimately proved true.) As buildings rose around it, the old house, with its worn porch and crooked chimney, just sat there.

I enjoyed this relic from the past, imagining it sitting there in June 1906, when my grandmother was born in her family's apartment only eight blocks away at 1403 Avenue A. On the next page is a photo of my great-grandmother, Giovanna Cuccia, with family members sitting in front of their fruit stand at the southwest corner of 75th Street and Avenue A (later named York Avenue in honor of Sargent Alvin York, a World War I hero). Giovanna, third from the right, is eight months pregnant with my grandmother.

It looks like anyone's old photo, but it led to a bona fide miracle a month after it was taken because Nan, Anna Cuccia, was born with two birthdays, July 23rd and July 28th. I learned this astounding fact at age 10 when I went to my grandmother's house to see what was up.

"Hi, Nan."

"That's it?"

"I said hi!"

"Where's my 'Happy Birthday?' "

"I wished you happy birthday on the 23rd and made you a card. It's right there on top of the TV."

"Today is my birthday, too."

Involuntarily, my head started shaking. I was used to my grandmother's inquisitions but I didn't understand this one.

"Nan, I don't get it."

She explained.

Saveria Palermo, a midwife from Yorkville, delivered Nan in her family's apartment on July 23rd, 1906. But Saveria was lazy. When she filled out the Board of Health birth certificate the following Monday, July 30th, she used the same date, Saturday, July 28th, for all the babies she had delivered that week. That's why Nan had two birthdays, July 23rd and July 28th.

Neither Giovanna nor my great-grandfather, Antonino Cuccia, knew English, so they never fixed the certificate. And they always celebrated Anna's—Nan's—birthday twice.

She was the baby in the family and a spoiled brat. She told me that with pride.

Cuccia family, at their fruit stand, 1906.

Herman the German

*Our local barber loves his native land and he loves
to give us the dreaded crew cut. Kids wear
baseball caps all year round to hide the damage.*

At five after three, Michael, Steven, and Gerard turned the
corner, marching up the avenue in formation, hammering
their cardboard schoolbags in time against the concrete sidewalk. Reaching 85th Street, they saw Herman the German
leaning his body out of his barbershop doorframe, an eager
look on his face as he awaited his prey.

The Murphy kinder, 12, 10, and 8, were getting haircuts.
They faced their sentence defiantly, dropping their asses
hard into the three barber chairs.

Every eight weeks, Mr. Murphy stopped at the barbershop
on the way home from his Transit Authority job in Coney Island. He prepaid three haircuts—75 cents apiece with a quarter tip—and gave orders. "Herman, each boy's head should
resemble a village green—short, trim, tight."

Mr. Murphy had two inflexible haircut rules: First, no hair
should make contact with the boy's shirt. Second, the boy's
hair must be too short to pull.

Rule Two had once led the middle son, Steven, to grief.
During geography class in fourth grade at St. Joseph's,
which all the Murphy boys attended, Steven was entertaining two girls in the back row. Sister Maria caught this usually sharp boy off-guard. She crept down the aisle until her
shadow covered his head. With the girls entranced and under
his power, Steven—Paul McCartney cute—had no warning
when the nun went to her classic move, the hair pull with a
neat neck snap. She had mastered this maneuver on countless knuckleheads early in her career.

Sister Maria pounced, but when she tried to pull Steven's
hair she came up with nothing. Too short. She tried again.

Only air. She had a better chance of running away with Father Heidi for the weekend—her deepest secret desire, according to a recurring rumor in the school's hallways.

Furious, the nun slugged Steven in the forehead with her two-pounder "Daughter of Christ," ring. His head swung back, hitting the blackboard with a beautiful thud. Punching boys into submission was a respected tradition both at St. Joseph's and St. Stephen's, my school. They called it cleaning a kid's clock. Sister Maria, recovering from her dark moment, realized there might be an injury.

"How are you?"

"Huh?"

"How many fingers do you see?"

"Wha?"

Later, Steven collected compliments on the tattoo left by the nun's ring. For two days, if you wiped the sweat and dirt from his forehead, you could see the imprint of the ring's inscription.

The first time Mr. Murphy arranged for the triple haircut he came home and the boys were sitting at the dinner table. From the apartment's front door he immediately saw something was amiss.

"Do I see unacceptable hair lengths? Are you mocking me? There will be no mocking! Anita, hold dinner."

Frugal Mr. Murphy dropped his shopping bag full of on-sale irregular tube socks and ordered the boys back to Herman's. They arrived just as he was locking his door.

"Herman, these aren't the haircuts I asked for. I demand you fix them right now, or I want my money back, including the tip!"

Herman looked the boys up and down.

"Ach du lieber, Mr. Murphy, these boys look wunderbar!"

"Your ass'll look wunderbar if you don't open the door and cut their hair."

Deflated, Herman flipped the lock, hit the light and reached for his barber's smock. It hung from the hook under the Kaiser Wilhelm portrait.

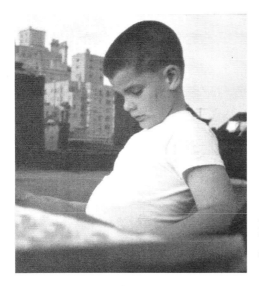

Reading—and sporting
both a Herman crew cut
and a future beer belly,
1962.

After the deed was done, Mr. Murphy nodded his approval, the boys pouted, and Herman dreamed of the day when all haircuts would be done once.

Every September Herman closed his store for the annual Steuben Day parade which honors Baron Friedrich von Steuben, the Revolutionary War hero who came to the aid of George Washington. The march ends in the center of Yorkville's German town. An early riser, Herman would put on his lederhosen, yodeling socks, short Von Trapp-style jacket, and an Alpine hat with a single feather. He'd run up 86th Street to secure a good position in front of the RKO movie house. There he'd stand on a milk box with a blue cornflower, a symbol of Germany, pinned to his lapel, and madly wave two German flags until the street sweepers followed the last band with their brooms.

Herman knew the words to every song. For weeks after the parade, if you were getting a haircut, Herman would sing "The Happy Wanderer" softly in your ear.

Herman's narrow shop was crammed between a bar and a beauty salon. He had no room near the entrance to plant a barber pole, so he hung a photo of a barber pole in his window. It looked stupid, but it helped block the view in or out.

This was important to me, because if the neighborhood's jerky kids saw you in the death chair, they'd storm the place and spread out to watch you get scalped—all angles covered to enhance the commentary. After a haircut, you always looked weird. The hyenas followed you home taunting all the way. Kids wore baseball caps year round to cover the damage. The barber pole photo, which offered at least some cover, was my friend.

Herman wore a monocle and had a shiny bald top with a buzz cut on the sides. It was comforting to think, as I sat in his barber chair, that at least he, too, had a crappy haircut. As Herman snipped away, a cigarette would dangle from his mouth, often coming dangerously close to my ear when he leaned in to work on my sides. I could feel the heat of the ash.

Herman wasn't actually visible during most of the haircut. A swirl of smoke enveloped my head. You only knew he was there by his smell; a cocktail of tobacco and talc. Sometimes the first thing coming out of the cloud was his monocle and his eye behind it, magnified like a horror movie.

Despite the dread of getting a haircut, it was fun sitting in the chair. I was truck-driver high and surveyed the store. If Herman turned the chair to the left, I might see a man thumbing through a Playboy in the "off limits to kids" waiting area. Even at that distance, the photos were delivered tout de suite to the room in my brain where my art collection hung on the walls. This was my favorite stop on my way to dreamland.

But one thing on Herman's counter bugged me a lot: the Butch-Stick display.

Butch-Stick was a waxy hair product that made your crew cut stand up in front like a lawn. First of all, I hated getting a crew cut. Girls wouldn't look at you. That there was this unique product to make a crew cut look better made no sense to me since I thought all crew cuts were bad ideas.

Adding insult, the product display included a picture of Yankee star Roger Maris with a bubble over his head saying, "I Use Butch-Stick!" Well, Roger, that's great, just what I needed. Every two months, I gave my father fifty reasons why it was not a good idea for me to get a crew cut. Dad's response: "If a crew cut is good enough for Roger Maris, well then it's certainly good enough for my son."

With all due respect—up yours, Maris.

But there was one reason I was glad to get a crew cut, and it had to do with the combs submerged in blue water in the glass jars. Under no circumstance did I want my Teutonic trimmer to pull one of those long combs out of the blue-water jars and put it to my head. If I had a crew cut there would be no reason to.

Why did I hate the blue-water combs? The answer requires a journey into the mind of a Yorkville kid.

We kids knew lots of things about Herman. We knew that he kept a liverwurst sandwich and an apple in a brown bag under a copy of the *Staats-Zeitung* newspaper in a drawer. We knew he had a Grundig shortwave radio. And we knew that Herman was fit. He practiced the gymnastic rings at the Turn Verein, a German-American social center, three times a week, and only bought lean meat at Schaller & Weber.

For us kids, there was one big mystery about Herman. As far as we knew, from the time he opened in the morning until the time he closed at night, he never left his shop to go the bathroom. We knew that Herman's shop had no plumbing beside the lone sink in front of the barber chairs where he washed his hands. That is, there was no bathroom. True, in the building next store there was a bathroom in the back of the first floor hallway, but we never saw him use it.

So how did Herman get through the day?

My friends and I suspected that the secret was hidden in the blue water. We believed that, if you looked in the barbershop window on Monday, the second and third comb jars were dry, but as the week progressed those jars would get fuller and fuller. If these were filling with pee, though, how did it turn blue? Our theory: On Mondays Herman would place a Ty-D-Bol tablet in the comb jar that sat on the counter next to the first barber chair, his chair of first resort. That was his go-to jar, and as it got filled he would pour the contents into jars two and three.

When Herman's need for a leak became unstoppable, we theorized he would stand at the window by the first barber chair and shut close the shoulder-high curtains. His eyes would dart, checking from side to side while he strategically centered himself behind the barber pole photo. Once hidden, he would take down the jar, whip out his bird, and obtain his relief.

We kids couldn't say we found definitive proof of our theory, but late one Saturday I was playing catch in front of the barber shop. Herman's head was resting on the curtain rod to the side of the barber pole photo. Through his monocle, I noticed his eye spinning around aimlessly. He looked like he was moaning. This was followed by a weak smile on his face. I waved at him, but he didn't wave back. Observing this brought back the only reason I was happy to have my crew cut—no combs, no blue water.

"Heads up!" Steve yelled.

I turned and chased the ball down the sidewalk, leaving Herman to his private moment.

Trading Cards

*Wherein I figure out why it is that I have 14 cards
of New York Yankee outfielder Hector Lopez
but not one of my favorite star.*

My obsession at eight was buying, trading, and flipping baseball cards. My collection fitted neatly inside a sturdy Converse sneaker box. The teams were in alphabetical order and the players were sorted by uniform number. I earned good money from my weekend candy-store job delivering newspapers. What's more; I had first crack at the baseball card deliveries each week since I knew the candy-store schedule. I could smell the gum as the cardboard boxes came off the truck. I hated gum, but oh boy, did I love Mickey Mantle. Inside the wrapper, under one of those fat pieces of gum, was a 1962 Topps card No. 200—Mickey Mantle. I had to have it.

"Please dear God, let there be a Mickey in here," I would pray just before peeling the cellophane off a pack. I'd slowly turn back the seal, hoping to see a pinstripe uniform—a Yankee. My eyes would dart to the bottom right edge of the card to see if there was an "OF," indicating that the player was an outfielder (like Mickey) and then to the spot just over the OF, looking for an "E," the final letter in his last name. No other Yankee name ended in E in 1962. I died every time I looked through a pack and found no Mickey. I knew exactly what his card looked like because I had seen a photo of it in a sports magazine.

Hector Lopez? Him I had. Fourteen of him! Thirteen more than I needed. I never found a Mickey card. I had a better chance of dating Hayley Mills. My card collecting peaked in 1964 and started sputtering in 1965. Getting older and wiser, I recognized the scam the card companies were running—dropping one All-Star player into every 20,000 cards they printed, so we poor jerks kept coming back. Plus, my money was being redirected to my new-found love, record collecting.

But I still loved the Yankees, and by the end of school in 1966, when I was 12, I began sneaking off to weekday Yankee games alone. I wasn't officially allowed on the subway, but as long as I was home for dinner no one questioned my whereabouts. My family assumed I was at P.S. 158 for summer day camp. A pretty good deal, but I liked to break it up occasionally with a Yankee game. I preferred going solo to the Stadium because it lowered the odds that I'd get caught in my custom of staying there long after the game had ended and everyone else had gone home.

The Stadium was big and quiet when it was empty, and distant sounds circled the place under the stands. One time, a rent-a-cop called "The Major"—the same nickname as Ralph Houk, the Yankee manager—spotted me and tried to chase me. He was the head of the meager Yankee security team. He wore a baggy suit, limped, and dragged his leg a bit. He looked older than my grandfather and talked mean. "What I tell you? Get out!"

The chances were low that the Major would ever catch me, but I didn't want to press my luck. I learned to avoid him by hiding in the bathroom at the end of the lower level in left field. There would be other kids hiding there, too, whom I didn't know. After each game the Major would check every bathroom in the Stadium to see that it was empty. Starting in the right field grandstands, he'd work his way around the three levels, and then finish his search in lower left field. This gave us plenty of time to screw around, then at the right time go into the bathroom. Exhausted from searching three levels, the Major never came all the way into that last bathroom. He just stuck his head through the door and craned his neck around. We stood on the toilets and held our breath. Once he was gone, the place was ours.

We ran onto the field and touched the monuments. I rubbed Lou Gehrig's face until my hand blistered. We slid into second base and rolled around on the foul-line chalk. Getting up, we looked like survivors from a flour factory explosion. Who cared? And that wasn't the best part—the best part was going into the dugout to sit in their seats—Ruth, Gehrig, DiMaggio, Ford, and Mantle—they all sat there, and we did, too.

One day, playing around in the dugout after a Red Sox game, four of us slowly walked down the tunnel that led to the players' locker rooms. We heard voices, and then saw players coming out of the Red Sox clubhouse, some with bottles of beer, most smoking cigarettes, and all of them with wet hair. They were on their way to the team bus which was parked in the left field bullpen with it's motor running. Security wasn't interested in the Boston players but we were, and we wanted every autograph. We only had one game program and fought over it, ripping it to pieces, one for each kid. The boy who owned the program was miserable. I had my own Bic pen. We descended on the players.

Reggie Smith, the outfielder signed for me first, and then Mel Parnell, the Red Sox announcer and former lefty pitcher. He went 25–7 in 1949 and started in that year's All-Star game. I loved lefties; I'm a lefty. After a player signed, I swung back to catch the next guy. My targets included Tony Conigliaro, Rico Petrocelli, and Ken, "The Hawk," Harrelson. Their signatures ran over each other, but I didn't care. After most of the players exited, it was obvious one was still in there: Carl Yastrzemski, their MVP. When Yaz appeared he was carrying a suit over one shoulder and had a cigarette in his free hand. The other kids surrounded him. I watched.

"Carl, Carl, please sign my paper!" Each of them said this with little variation.

Yaz grunted "No" and briskly walked away.

The guys tried one more time. "Carl! Carl!"

This time he turned. "Go away!"

I waited a few seconds, letting him build distance, and then I ran after him with soft steps until I was alongside him, just him and me.

"Mr. Yastrzemski, congratulations on your homer and win today."

In my Yorkville Stars gear in Carl Schurz Park.

The ballplayer gave me a brief warm look that quickly turned back into a scowl. I hated the Red Sox, gulped and said, "My family's from Long Island." I lied. He was from Southampton.

"Where?" he asked.

"Montauk." We were feet from the team's bus and I blurted out, "Can I please have your autograph?"

"I don't sign."

"Why? It makes no sense. What are you going to do with it? Save it for when you're an old man?"

He put his cigarette out under his shoe and loosened his necktie. "Go play, kid; it's a nice day out." He got on the bus and the door closed.

On the subway ride home, I wished Yastrzemski a hitless rest of the season, and then remembered I had to drop by my grandmother's to pick up knitting wool for my mother. When I got there, Nan Rode and her sister, Aunt Mary, were arguing over the wake cards of their recently dead cousin, Father Louie.

"I have only two, I can't give you one," Nan said.

"He was our last living first cousin, Annie!" Mary said.

"Sorry, Mary, I need a backup."

"Come on!"

"Nope."

If you don't know what a wake card is, here's a definition: At a Catholic wake, to thank you for coming to the funeral home, the grieving family dispenses little plastic holy cards. They have a Catholic image on one side and, on the other, the name, birth date, and date of demise of the deceased. Sometimes a prayer is thrown in free of charge. They're like wedding favors, but different.

Old Catholic ladies carried wake cards in their handbags the way that 10-year-old boys filled their pockets with baseball cards and marbles. The number you owned showed how many wakes you attended and lifted your piety rating. (My grandmother had more than 50.) If the rivalry got vicious, the bags' contents would be dumped onto the kitchen table and the wake cards would be separated from the hundred other sundries and examined for both quantity and quality.

The following week, I overheard three ladies in a heated discussion in front of St. Stephen's Rectory. Mrs. Reilly and Mrs. Muller desperately wanted one of Mrs. Cupo's extra Father Kevin cards. The beloved priest had died tragically while reaching down from the 79th Street curb to retrieve his "pick me up" flask. It had fallen into the gutter. An older driver, low behind the steering wheel, failed to see the wee priest, and knocked him a block up to Second Avenue.

Unfortunately, I was late for altar boy duty and missed the outcome of the ladies' debate. As I walked away I dreamed that Mantle's baseball card was safely tucked away in my sock drawer. That trance broke and left me feeling angry. Soon another fantasy took its place. I saw an older Yaz stepping off a curb to pick up his flask as a little old lady raced her car toward the yellow traffic light, hoping to beat its switch to red. Yaz was right in her path.

Mickey Mantle

*The immortal No. 7 is standing two feet
away from me. Will I freeze in the clutch?*

Number 7, the New York Yankees' amazing centerfielder,
stood two feet away from me at the 86th Street RKO Theater in April 1962. The team had made a silly movie, *Safe at
Home*, to capitalize on the heroics of Roger Maris and Mickey Mantle in the 1961 home run derby. The following spring
the players visited several New York City movie houses to
promote the film. William Frawley, aka Fred Mertz of *I Love
Lucy* fame, was the only real actor I remember being in the
picture.

I finagled Dad to go to the theater two hours early to make
sure we got the best seats. Before we went inside, we had
a quick burger across the street at Prexy's. Then, with me
pulling Dad's hand, we entered the lobby and I asked an
usher what side the Yankees would be coming down. "Right
aisle," he said. Around seven o'clock, word spread that the

With Dad and Red Murphy outside Loftus Tavern, 1966.

team bus had pulled up in front. The Yankees came into the lobby dressed in dark suits, white shirts, and dark ties. They marched down the right side of the movie house where we had stationed ourselves. Yogi Berra walked past me and stepped on my toe. I didn't notice, though my father did, and from the look on his face, Dad wanted Berra to apologize. It was strange seeing Dad pissed at Yogi, a three-time MVP.

When the line came to a halt, Elston Howard stopped directly in front of me and put his arms behind his back like a military M.P. Ellie saw I was near having a baby because Mickey Mantle was standing right next to him—two feet away from me. I was shaking in my sneakers. I heard Dad and Ellie exchange laughs over my dilemma, so Howard leaned over toward me and whispered, "Say hi, kid. He won't bite you." But I was too scared to say anything. I watched my opportunity walk away from me a moment later when the team proceeded onto the stage for a final bow before the crappy film began. Even at age 8, I knew I was watching a box office flop.

Five years later, in May 1967, I forced Dad to take me to three straight Yankee games after Mantle hit his 499th homer. I was going to catch number 500. The Mick would smash it into the right field grandstands (I knew it, I just knew it), and that's where we sat Friday night, Saturday afternoon, and Sunday afternoon for the entire Baltimore Orioles series. I brought my glove to every game.

Well, he didn't hit it Friday night, and it drove my father nuts that the Yankees were down by 12 runs in the eighth inning—Hal Reniff gave up nine runs—and I still wouldn't leave. I had to see every Mick at bat. He didn't hit No. 500 on Saturday either. But God bless Stu Miller, the Baltimore Oriole pitcher. On Sunday he threw a meatball to Mantle and The Mick clocked it. That ball was coming straight to me and I could feel the hair on my father's neck stand up, forget mine. I watched the ball soar over the first baseman, then travel most of the outfield at the height of our grandstand seats, and then, like a broken balloon, start to fall and fall into the lower right field seats. My excitement slipped for a second, I wasn't going to catch it, but Mickey hit 500! Mickey hit 500! Mickey hit 500! Dad and I hugged and cheered ourselves hoarse right through the next batter. Our legs were rocky.

After the season, I wrote Mickey a letter asking for an autograph. I wrote it out once, Mom corrected it in pencil, and then I re-wrote it. I mailed that copy with a stamped, self-addressed envelope. Five months later, I received a picture of Mantle with a phony signature. I traced real ink over his name and made believe he signed it. I kept it forever.

It's Not a Blouse!

Church bowling, and other tales of the altar-boy life.

"Bob, I need more house money," Mom said.

"Why?" Dad asked.

"To clean Tommy's surplices."

"His what?" Dad said, frantically looking for his keys and belt.

"Surplices… the things he wears serving Mass."

"Oh, you mean the blouses?"

I cringed. Rory laughed.

"They're not blouses." Mom gave me a supportive look. We exchanged foolish smiles.

"They sure look like blouses. Cleaning blouses is a house expense. It should come out of your house money."

The Pryor men, near St. Stephen's, 1963.

Dad wasn't keen about my altar boy and choir duties. He told Mom that the whole thing was a little odd.

"They're not blouses, but if they were, that's not the issue. You haven't put a dime more into house expenses in the last three years." Mom shook her head and added, "If you decided to smoke four packs of cigarettes a day instead of three, wouldn't that change how much money you spend on cigarettes?"

"Your point?" Dad had never seen me serve Mass or sing in the choir. I never saw him in church outside of our first communions and confirmations.

After a deep breath, Mom continued, "If Tommy needed a new baseball glove, would you buy it for him?"

"Why? What happened to his old one?" Dad ran out the door, late for work, with his belt rolled up in his hand.

Every time I walked into the apartment with a dirty surplice Mom's face dropped. I'm sure she was thinking about my father's brick skull. The pressure was on me to keep them clean. If they didn't pass Brother Albert's muster he'd send them back home and Mom would have a fit over the embarrassment and having to spend another 35 cents for cleaning.

Nobody made me become an altar boy, I wanted to. It allowed me to work on my spiritual balance sheet, just as being in the choir and being a Boy Scout helped make up for my idiot streak. I knew I was going to be bad and I needed something as an offset. There was a chance I was going to Hell; Sister Lorraine and Mrs. Francis told me that all the time. I needed to change my salvation ticket to Purgatory, or better yet, Limbo, for a heatless stay.

I was also trying to perfect my faith in the mysteries and rituals of the Mass. I wanted it all to be true. But I couldn't resist trouble, even while wearing my surplice. When I had to serve a funeral, I rarely got a tip and there were no friends in the church to torture me. This was boring. One funeral, on Holy Saturday as it happened, started late because the hearse had a flat. To kill time, Smithy, the other altar boy, and I heard each other's confession in the shadowy booth used for that sacrament.

"Forgive me, Father, for I have sinned," I said. "I killed my nun, kicked my father in the ass, and knocked over Joe's Candy Store."

Smithy offered me absolution. "You are forgiven, my son. For penance, say three Hail Mary's and sneeze five times in your grandmother's hankie."

Brother Albert gave out the altar boy assignments every Friday at 2 p.m. (a reason to get out of class!). I would run the freshly inked mimeograph sheet under my nose, making myself light-headed, then I would quickly scan the light purple print looking for my name, praying that I'd see it next to a wedding and dreading that I'd see it next to an early morning Mass instead. (The only plus for doing the early Mass was the chance to see and get a smile from Don Ameche, a St. Stephen's regular and a famous movie actor who played Alexander Graham Bell, D'Artagnan and many others.) The older, brown-nosing altar boys got the best assignments, the young wiseguys like myself did the worst. Most of my assignments were early, or the all-time worst assignment after the Vatican moved away from Latin: the 10 o'clock Mass on Sunday in Hungarian. What the hell were they saying?

That was Father Emeric's Mass. He was a nice guy, but once he got into his Hungarian groove, English flew out the window. He'd forget I knew only English and would give me directions in Hungarian; I'd stare at him waiting for sign language or his miraculous recovery back into English. This Mass was a long event, with everyone drunk on nationalism.

On the Holy Saturday that the hearse had a flat, after Smithy and I finished our phony confessions, I ran straight into the sacristy to change for the funeral without realizing I really had to pee badly. But I had no time, and there was no bathroom! As I buttoned up my cassock from my neck to my feet, I checked the door and the passageway. The coast was clear. I hoisted my cassock and peed into the slop sink.

"Hey!"

A voice startled me. I quickly put myself away. Then I turned and saw Mr. Goody Two-Shoes, otherwise known as Steve Nemeth, an eighth-grade pain-in-the-ass on his way to a career as either a priest or a prison guard. He hadn't decided which yet.

"What!" I asked.

"You will burn in hell for urinating in God's house."

Anything I might say would be pointless.

"Well," he asked, "what do you have to say for yourself?"

I held my ground, said nothing, and washed my hands.

"With soap, lots of soap. You must not soil the Lord's vessels," he said.

I held my hands up, showed Nemeth they were clean, and gave him the finger when he turned around.

After the funeral, I ran home to change. Dad was getting up and I asked him if he wanted to go for a bike ride. He said no, but how about a catch? I waited for him on the stoop, throwing the Spaldeen against the side of a car. Walking over to Loftus Tavern, we talked.

"Tommy, why are you in the choir?"

"I like to sing."

"I've never heard you sing except through the door of the bathroom."

"I only do it in crowds."

Dad gave me his "I-can't-figure-you-out" look, and walked to the other side of 85th Street. We played catch over the cars for an hour. I went to the park and Dad went to the tavern.

There was an Easter vigil that night with a full Mass. All the kids in school were encouraged to attend because the second graders, who were making their first communion, would wear their new blue suits and ruffled white dresses. The nuns wanted us to support them. Many of my friends turned this into a social event; it gave us a destination to get out of the chilly April rain. The church was packed, and there was no room to sit, so we stood in the back, avoiding the ushers who tried to shove us into a pew.

During parts of a Mass, everyone in church had to kneel, including the people standing in the back. They usually knelt on one knee. Sometimes, there were as many as a dozen kids kneeling, all lined up. They moaned and complained, moving from one knee to the other on the cold marble floor until it was time to stand again. If most were on one knee, with the correct force I could knock all of them over with one good shove. I watched for my opportunity. I stepped three steps away from the first kneeler and then ran into him as hard as I could. I started counting the tumblers. This was Church Bowling! The record was thirteen down. I never made it past nine. But I wasn't hung up on the record. I simply loved listening to the grunts and groans as each kid hit the next, a beautiful ballet, with body after body going down—like dominos. It was important to seem detached afterward to deter detection. I got lost. Smithy later confirmed my score for the frame was eight.

The next day was Easter. An altar boy got sick, and I ended up getting the juicy nine o'clock children's Mass. Full house! Everybody was there and I loved playing my role in the ancient ceremonies and rituals. On special occasions, I added a trick of my own.

Twice during a Mass, the altar boy rings a set of heavy gold-plated bells held together by a large screwed-on handle. Each priest had different bell preferences. Some liked snappy hard rings, others favored softer tolling. Toward the end of this Easter Mass, I worked the screw on the bell handle down to a precarious half turn and left it there. I waited around the back of the church for the ten o'clock Hungarian Mass. When it began, I saw that the altar boy was my personal Satan, Steve Nemeth.

This is where the priest's ringing preference made a world of difference in the quality of my trick. If the priest wanted a short solemn ring, the bells would simply fall off the handle. "Oops! Sorry." But, if the priest wanted loud tolling, the altar boy would lift the bells to the sky—like a town crier—and on the first whip of his arm, the bells would fly off the altar towards the pews.

"Incoming!"

The old ladies would duck like players who stand too close to the cage during batting practice at Yankee Stadium.

Unfortunately, Father Emeric, a quiet man who preferred light action, was celebrating the Mass. Nemeth rang the bells. They broke away, leaving him holding the handle as the five chimes clattered across the marble altar, coming to rest when they hit the pulpit.

When I got home, Dad was at the kitchen table eating a bowl of corn flakes. Mom and Rory had left the house to help Nan Ryan with Easter dinner.

"I saw you in church last night," Dad said.

"Huh?" I said, stunned.

"We ate out, at the Silver Moon. On our way over there, Mom said, "Let's pop in to church," so we did. We figured you'd be up in the choir; I looked there, but didn't see you. Then, I saw you standing in the back with your friends. Why weren't you singing?"

I sighed with relief. He obviously had missed the church bowling match.

"I was late and the nun won't let you sing if you're not on time."

"Choir sounded nice," Dad said. He put his spoon down and asked, "How many girls are in the choir?"

"Fifteen."

"How many boys?"

"Three."

Dad smiled, picked up his spoon and swept it through his bowl.

Mrs. Sweeney Sure Is Old

*She and Mickey have a long talk
at the flower shop about the Grand Central Parkway.
Or maybe it's about something else.*

I felt delighted when I left the church after sabotaging the altar bells on Steve Nemeth that it didn't even bother me when Brother Albert cornered me exiting through the girls' entrance. This was forbidden.

"Thomas, how are you this morning?"

"I'm fine, Brother."

"Good, very good. I need a favor. Go to the store and pick up a dozen roses. Here's two dollars."

I figured I got off easy, and asked Brother Albert to hold my surplice. He made a face, but took the hanger. I walked

Cherokee Democratic Club, 334 East 79th Street, 1962.

144

to the flower shop on 84th Street and First Avenue. Mickey the florist was taking care of a customer when I walked in. "Tommy, be with you in five minutes."

Mrs. Sweeney was buying a tombstone floral arrangement for a visit to her parents' grave later that morning. She planned to take the Grand Central instead of the Long Island Expressway based on Mickey's suggestion. Mrs. Sweeney also said her back had been acting up, and she wasn't as young as she used to be and felt old.

"Oh, no you're not," said Mickey.

"I'm old," Mrs. Sweeney answered, as she tossed her wavy hair around.

"Your legs say otherwise." Mickey smiled.

I learned all this while a five-minute wait drifted into fifteen minutes. The Grand Central Parkway may have been a smart idea, but as to Mrs. Sweeney's age, Mickey needed glasses. My eyes saw a 35-year-old, lumpy, over-the-hill mother of three.

With Father Dudley, N.Y. Giants chaplain.

After the sale and the long goodbye (I thought they'd kiss), Mickey came over to me and made small talk. "So how is your grandmother? Is she running for re-election this year?"

"Yes, she is," I said with a forced smile. Since Nan Rode was a local politician, all my comings and goings were reported back to her faster than jungle drums.

"Mickey, Brother Albert says he needs a dozen roses pronto! Here's two dollars."

"That's odd, it's Easter—no weddings, no funerals…and two dollars isn't enough for nice roses. OK, I'll get the flowers, and I'll put it on the church's tab."

I was frantic—more than 25 minutes for a two-block errand. I was dead. I ran like a madman, turned down the block, and saw Brother Albert standing under the massive St. Stephen of Hungary cross. His arms were folded tightly; his brown leather sandal tapped the concrete as I ran toward him.

"Where have you been—and what are *those*?"

"I went to Mickey's. Here are your roses."

I passed the flowers to Brother Albert and his face twisted as though the bouquet was a stinky diaper.

"Roses? Roses? Pastor Dudley and three angry priests with cold coffee are waiting for bakery rolls upstairs. Roses? My God! Here, take your blouse."

"It's *not* a blouse!" I said.

Incoming!

Boom! A manhole cover goes airborne. It might land harmlessly in the street. Or it might land on Pete Palermo's beloved patrician green Thunderbird convertible.

It was a lazy, warm evening, in early June 1965. I was sitting on my stoop staring at my incredibly dirty sneakers and talking to Paddy McNamara.

"School's winding down," I said.

"It's light out until nearly nine o'clock," Paddy answered.

We grinned. Our heads bobbed up and down in rhythm and that reminded me of the bobble-head dog that sat in the back window of Pop Rode's Plymouth before Rory and I broke it. When the car moved, the boxer's head bobbed and I would sing this song, "When the Red, Red Robin (Comes Bob, Bob, Bobbin' Along)."

My grandfather joined in unless someone cut him off. That happened often.

June nights made me dreamy.

"Are you going to Ten Mile River scout camp in July?" I asked Paddy.

"All depends."

An explosion stopped our conversation.

Down the street, a manhole cover went airborne, flipping like a coin. It hit peak height at a third-floor fire escape and then plummeted—smashing through the white cloth top of Pete Palermo's patrician green 1964 Thunderbird convertible, and landing on its candy-striped rear seats.

"Shit!" Paddy and I said.

Several windows flew open and heads popped out like in an Italian opera. Through one window, I saw Adeline, Pete's pretty blonde wife, poke her head out. As soon as she saw it was her car, her eyes opened wide. A split second later, her husband pulled her off the windowsill by her neck, then

The dreaded 83rd Street gang, 1965.

lunged so far out the fourth floor window I was sure he was either going to jump or fall. After a law-of-self-preservation adjustment, Pete went to a window with a fire escape, jumped on the landing, and zoomed down the outside of the building. He slipped off the second-floor emergency ladder as fast as a monkey spying a fat banana. He circled his car three or four times, all the while holding both hands up against his cheeks so hard I thought he was going to push his lips off his face. His hair was perfect.

"Hey, look, doesn't he look like he's saying, "Mamma mia, Mamma mia?" Paddy held his face the same way.

"This is so good," I said.

"Oh no, no, no, no, no, no," Pete said. He was a basket case. Pete loved his car, his comb, his straight white teeth, his casual-dress sweater collection, his wife, and his son in that order. His best friend was the last mirror he passed. Being on the top step of my stoop, Paddy and I had front row seats for all the action. We continued taking furious mental notes.

Slowly, other men moved in to lend Pete support.

"Ooooh, wow, Pete, what a shame."

"Do you think a steam pipe burst?"

"Noooo.... I think the manhole was running away from home," said Paddy's father, Paddy Senior, confusing sarcasm with what he called "fine Irish humor."

The mob gave Pete the necessary distance.

Then someone said, "Maybe we should get that thing out of there."

After one of the convertible's doors was opened, four men leaned in to remove the manhole cover.

Pete pleaded, "Easy, easy, Jesus Christ, easy."

Feeling sorry for him, the guys readjusted their handling, adding soft, touching, dramatic moves to their effort. A classic religious statue came to my mind.

"Don't drag it—lift it completely off the seat and watch the upholstery!" Pete said.

"Shit, Allie! Clean your feet! I just shampooed the rug yesterday."

Allie scraped his soles and heels against the curb's edge out of respect. The four men were not wearing black suits but they resembled pallbearers. They lifted the manhole cover with dignity and propped it up against the bottom three steps of the closest stoop. Pete, motionless by the car for a few minutes, said nothing but then muttered a series of low curses I couldn't make out. Then, he spun to face the manhole cover, yelling several times in chicken-clucking style, "Fuck, fuck, fuck, fuck, fuck…"

Finally, he gave the manhole cover a couple of solid kicks, until it slipped down the steps. It made a metal-on-concrete swooshing sound that echoed across the wall of buildings, then slammed to the sidewalk with a thud. Pete wore soft leather Italian shoes with no socks, so his face switched from a look of spiritual pain to one of intense physical pain. He was helped to an adjacent stoop by two guys, each taking one of his arms. Pete took his shoe off and started rubbing his damaged foot. Before he sat, he brushed the stoop for noticeable dirt.

Paddy and I looked at each other. It was going to be a great summer.

Street Rides

*The secret to a satisfying bumper-car collision
is to be the third man in.*

Beginning mid-June, two street rides would show up at night
after dinner: Bumper Cars and the Half Moon. Each ride sat
on a flat-bed truck; the driver doubled as the ride operator.
He'd park at a hydrant opening. Admission was a dime.
My daily allowance was three dimes. No ifs, ands, or buts—
three dimes. That was it. To get on these rides I gave up a
lot of good stuff: Drake's and Hostess cakes, records, comics, soda, balsam airplane gliders, or wax candy. These rides
forced me off the dole, driving me to my first job, at eight
years of age, delivering newspapers. I needed my stuff and I
needed those rides.

Often, my friends and I would wait on a stoop for the rides
to come. With our elbows on our knees and our hands on our
chins, we would stare down the block toward the river, waiting for the ride to turn off East End Avenue.

**The Cisco Kid
rides again,
Lamston's, 1957.**

The bumper cars were just like the bumper cars at an amusement park except the cars were smaller and the circular track was the size of a tiny apartment. There were five cars and if you were a fat kid it was no use trying to squeeze yourself into one. When a chubby kid got stuck, the operator got aggravated, so he usually eyed the big ones up and down and sometimes wouldn't let them on. Time was money and he had other blocks to get to. The good news was that the small cars worked to a little kid's advantage since you could actually see where you were going once the ride started up. The only problem was the track size. Once the five cars were occupied, the operator lined them up, stepped off the track, and switched on the electricity. Then the cars began moving, and he'd watch his watch. Seven minutes. Never longer, never shorter.

He did nothing if cars got tangled up, as they often did on the tiny track. "I ain't no wrestling referee," he'd say. So sometimes you spent seven minutes piled all together and yelling at each other, "Get moving, doofus!" or "Blockhead, you're turning the wheel the wrong way," or "Dummy, forward!"

It was virtually impossible to put any distance between my car and whomever I wanted to bump, making it difficult to get the proper speed or angle for a solid broadside or an efficient rear-ender. Ideally, I wanted to be the third man in, right after two of my rivals had whacked each other. They'd be recovering from whiplash and yelling—completely ignorant of my proximity. This allowed stretched-out moments of glorious anticipation before I slammed them silly. There's talent in being able to post your vehicle toward the perfect impact point while simultaneously remaining deeply focused on your victim's head, shoulders, and neck. My heart soared if, pre-impact, the victim flashed a look of terror, knowing it was me who would deliver fresh pain. The cherry on top was my victim shooting me a look of grudging respect: "I acknowledge the precision of your attack."

When the bumper car ride left, everybody would sit on a stoop, regroup, and check up on injuries. No liniment was available or offered. All agreed it was a fine battle if one's head lolled a little to the side, maybe resting a noggin gently on the stoop's railing to take a bit of weight off the neck. At times, my head felt like a bowling ball on a pencil.

The Bumper Cars guy was in cahoots with the Half Moon guy. I knew it because they never showed up on the same night. The Half Moon was a vomit machine that resembled a baby's cradle, a swing ride with four tiers of seats facing each other on each side. Each row had room for about four kids and a broom-thin bar, a useless source of support.

The Half Moon was powered by the operator's elbow grease. He would grab the side of the ride and begin rocking the kid-filled cradle. Once it was in motion, momentum helped the operator the same way it helps when you push a kid on a swing. He would send the ride higher and higher until it flirted with 90 degrees and many children feared it was going to flip over and threatened to relocate their dinners. I loved the roar of the kids' "whoa's" with every dip and rise as the Half Moon swung back and forth.

Anyone who sat in the first row at the bottom was considered a pussy. Sitting in the second row, you avoided taunts. If you sat in the third row you were OK with everyone, even the nut cases and bullies. If you sat in the fourth row at the very top, not only did you get a free pass with the bullies and nut cases (usually sitting next to you), but you also earned points with the girls. Blind, hapless desperation for female adoration drove many a boy up the metal Everest to his sure doom. Put me in that group.

There was a rumor started by the older guys that, in the late 1950s, a Half Moon operator despondent over a break-up with his longtime girlfriend forgot to evenly balance the weight and number of kids on each side of the ride. He sent the ride well past 90 degrees and it flipped over. Seven kids supposedly went airborne and a few switched sides. Kids got off the ride a little loopy and bumped into hydrants, light poles and cars. But except for a few cuts and bruises, everyone survived.

Top row, nut cases only!

The rumor-mongering teenagers also told us that the City Council decided, after careful deliberation, to let the ride continue operation if a safety chain was installed across each row of the ride. This safety chain had the same thickness and strength as one of those plastic key chains you'd weave on a boring rainy day at the pavilion in Carl Schurz Park. Depending on the mood of the kid nearest the hook end of the chain, it either stayed on or off. The majority of riders preferred bareback.

Unlike the Bumper Cars, where direct damage to a chum or foe was straightforward, the Half Moon presented subtle challenges. I could bump someone in mid-swing, or I could try to loosen their death grip on the safety bar. This was particularly gratifying when I saw the blood leave my neighbor's face. I developed other sneaky tortures.

When I'm excited, I dribble. I realized that this presented an opportunity. Gravity would take my spit on a journey directly to the other side's fourth tier. Since the fourth tier was always packed, somebody would always get wet. At first, it was easy to look innocent. And since it was just a little spit and always slipped out of the side of my mouth, it was nearly impossible for the guy on the other side to tell if it was me or not. Plus, I learned a few tricks:

Keys to a Perfect Hit

- Never make eye contact with your victim.
- Under no circumstances let the target suspect you through your outward gloating and selfish need to celebrate a direct hit.
- Confirm success only by aural means, such as your victim's *"What the fuck?"* If the target sounds particularly shocked, the odds are high that you hit a point of vulnerable entry—an eye, nostril or, God willing, his mouth.
- Consider planting false clues, especially if you are sitting next to a numb-nuts. You could give him a good poke in the ribs as you let the spit fly. Your victim might be led to believe that guy going through the monkey moves was the spitter.

On the day of the flying manhole cover, Paddy and I heard tires screech and saw the Half Moon guy racing through a yellow traffic light, turning his truck up 83rd Street with his loudspeaker blasting "Bits and Pieces" by the Dave Clark Five. Kids on the block yelped, "Ma, throw me a dime!" I had made a buck-twenty the previous day delivering newspapers for Joe's Candy Store, so Paddy and I were good to go.

But a minute later, as everyone was scrambling like an air-raid siren had sounded, I heard Frankie Valli singing. "Dawn, Go Away."

"The bumper cars!" kids screamed.

"Holy shit! Both rides!" Paddy said, rubbing his hands together.

This was a first. Somebody screwed up on the drivers' alternating business arrangement, and both of them were pissed. It rained the three previous days, and I guess that messed up their schedules. It was fun watching these red-faced guys in guinea T-shirts screaming and throwing their fat arms around like windmills. The second ride's arrival had put the block into a frenzy, with loopy kids now asking for two dimes most windows were being slammed shut by fed-up mothers.

Paddy and I watched and smiled. We knew we were going on *both* rides.

Murder by Dusting

*Mom murders Jerry Mahoney, our beloved
ventriloquist dummy. And it's just her opening salvo.*

Dad used to play a game with us: "If you could have one thing in the world, what would it be?"

Rory wanted his own TV. Not bad, that might have been my choice, too, but you had to pick your own thing. I chose a box seat at Yankee Stadium for baseball and football. Dad, a sailboat, no surprise. Mom never wavered. "I want my own room."

Mom ran her hand through her hair and said, "Relatives always lived with us. I had to split a bed with Joan. The only doors in the apartment were the bathroom and the front one, just like here."

Here Mom shot Dad a look, then continued, "We were six, without the extras. 'Every man for himself,' my father loved to say. Problem was, there were four girls in the house. I had to hide my few favorite things."

**Mom in dreamland
on 83rd Street
couch, 1962.**

Dad's art junk got on Mom's nerves. He painted, sketched, and sculpted. Clay freaked her out because it dug into fabric and was nearly impossible to completely remove.

"Bob, I'm going to kill you."

"What? Why?"

"Your clay, canvases, and paintbrushes are everywhere. I'm going nuts and I can't breathe in here. Between the dust, your crap, and the kids' crap, something's gotta give. I live with three sloppy pigs. I'm out of patience, we need a house!"

When Dad saw Mom losing it, he'd give Rory and me a look, and the three of us would tidy up the living room. Dad put his stuff behind the couch and Rory and I shoved ours under our bunk bed. This barely made a dent. We favored mess, Mom demanded clean. War was imminent. It started with Jerry.

"Give him the friggin' dummy, or you're dead."

I looked Mom in the eye and knew my negotiations with Rory were over. I handed him the Jerry Mahoney ventriloquist dummy, and he gave me his Knucklehead Smiff. Rory's face had a look of triumph that I quickly extinguished with a rap to his head when Mom turned away to resume making spaghetti. I left the kitchen before he snitched.

The dummies from the *Winchell-Mahoney Time* TV show were Christmas presents the year we turned five and seven. Rory immediately had a problem with Knucklehead. He looked goofy, and the name didn't sit well with Rory. I agreed, but played stupid, and made like Rory got the better of the deal by telling him that Knucklehead was a laugh riot and Jerry was boring. Not true, Jerry was cool, but I had to head Rory off. Sometimes, he believed me, but then he'd start to look Knucklehead over, check out my slick Jerry Mahoney and begin his act. Dad's nickname for Rory was Weepy. He went well past whine when he didn't like something—deep, heaving sobs, lots of physical stage work and, his best move, dropping to the floor when things weren't going his way. One night, he refused to go to bed. Mom kept dragging him into our bedroom, but five minutes later he'd sneak back out to the side of the couch and lay on the rug watching TV. Finally, Mom said to Dad, "Kick him in!"

Rory and I practiced our ventriloquist skills at the kitchen table during meals. Talking out of the side of our mouths, we had nonsensical conversations without variation or color that drove Mom loopy.

"How are you today, Jerry?"

"Just fine, Knucklehead. How are you today?"

"Fine, Jerry."

By the end of January, Mom wanted the dummies dead. She had a rule on toys—when they broke, they went in the garbage. It was only a matter of time.

Rory despised vegetables, especially wax beans and French-style string beans. Since we weren't allowed to leave food on our plates, the meal hour stretched as Rory sat there staring at his undesirables, trying to wait Mom

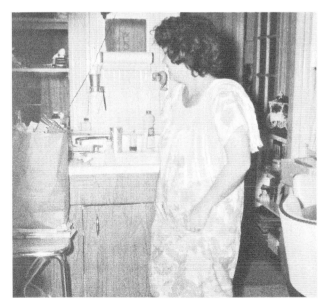

Mom near Jerry Mahoney's grave site.

out. Sometimes he won, sometimes he lost, all based on Mom's day and related mood. After we started bringing the dummies to the table, it didn't take long to figure out that the dummies were hollow and you could drop something in their mouths and down to their empty wood stomachs. Even though I wasn't crazy about vegetables, I had no desire to stick food in my dummy's mouth. Being a little older, I had a general idea how awful rotten food smelled. Rory didn't have this insight. Watching Mom and Dad carefully, he'd pick his openings and shovel the vegetable serving down the dummy's throat. I'd quietly encourage him, "Feed Jerry, Rory. Feed Jerry."

By the end of the second week, the science project in the dummy's stomach was in full swing, and the odor coming out of Jerry could've taken your eyebrows off. Dad caught the stench first. His face looked like he ate a sour ball, but Mom was the one who ripped the dummy off Rory's lap. She held Jerry's mouth to her nose, causing her to swoon and choke. When she recovered, Mom walked over to the stepladder and buried the dummy head first up to his waist in the brown paper garbage bag sitting on top of it. All I could see was Jerry's legs hanging over the top. I held Knucklehead tight and sang, "Hooray-Hoorah It's Winchell-Mahoney Time," the show's theme song, under my breath.

The dummy's swift death was part of Mom's campaign for a clutter-free home. Soon after, I asked her about my missing Phantom of the Opera model.

"Oh, I'm sorry honey, I was cleaning your room today and it was on the edge of your dresser. I accidentally knocked it over cleaning your stuff up." Mom said this without looking at me, continuing to wash down the kitchen wallpaper. Eventually, she turned, saw my face, and said, "It broke into so many pieces I had to throw it away."

"But I could've glued it all back together, that's how it started, as many pieces."

She stared at me for a long time, and then she recovered.

"Oh no, no, you'd never be able to repair it, it broke right across the Phantom's face."

I was speechless. As a talented liar, I recognized her story was false—this was a mob rubout. How could she? The Phantom was a favorite. It took two tubes of glue and five hours to put him together, and another three hours to paint him. The Phantom model had this unique feature at its base. A horrified little prisoner guy sticking his face through the bars of a dungeon's window built into a bank of rocks on a cliff. I knew that I had nailed the look of terror on the captive guy's face by painting his skin silver and white and making his teeth brownish and bloody.

This was just one of many "oops" accidents involving models. I lost Frankenstein, the Wolfman, a fighter plane, a frigate, and the all-time best model in the history of model-making, a foot-high replica of Yankee Stadium. It had bleachers, dugouts, and both bullpens right where they should be, in right and left fields. It had three tiers and the world famous Yankee Stadium roof overhang, with the copper façade detail that I painted white.

The day "The House that Ruth Built" disappeared, I went into shock.

I became a dog. I nosed every closet. Looked behind the couch, the chairs, and under the sink. My bone was not home.

"No, no, no, no, she wouldn't dare…she knows how much I love that thing…" I kept repeating this to myself over and over.

But it was true. Mom gave me her usual shovel of shit. "I was cleaning your dirty room and accidentally…" At some point, she grabbed both my arms and said squarely into my face, "I'm sorry, Hon. It's gone."

A fog of gloom crept over me. I stopped talking to Mom and didn't kiss her good night. She tried to win me back with hot chocolate and Drake's cakes. But, no, I tortured her by refusing desserts. In the second week of silence, after a long Saturday in the park, she put three unwrapped Yankee Doodles on a plate and an ice-cold quart of milk in front of me with a freshly washed glass clear of smudges.

Famished, I foolishly said, "Thanks, Mom," and gave in. From that point on, if Yankee Stadium came up in conversation, on the radio, on TV, Mom would break eye contact with me and start whistling through her teeth.

For Christmas in 1963, Rory's big gift was the Roman battleship, Big Caesar. The vessel was a notorious dust collector, doomed the moment it sailed into our harbor. It had moving parts, catapults, and two dozen sailors on the poop deck and below in the galley. Mom declared war on dust and completely ignored the Geneva Convention. All toy prisoners caught in enemy territory were shot on sight.

A month after Christmas, I was coloring at the kitchen table and Mom was cleaning our bedroom. She looked through the doorway to see if I was watching. I faked attention to my artwork and she returned to her cleaning. When she wasn't looking, I leaned over the table and snuck a peek into our bedroom. Feeling detection proof, she swung her arm up and swept Big Caesar off the dresser onto the floor, where she gave it a few kicks for good luck. I heard "Oops," followed by a quick nasty cough after the assassination.

Rory was less fazed about losing his stuff, but after Big Caesar's sinking, we formed an alliance against Mom. At 11 and 13, Rory and I still split the bunk bed in our tiny 83rd Street room. It was weird not trusting Mom. Protecting my remaining toys and games became an obsession. I kept them buried under my bed deep in the back, safe from her vacuuming assaults with her short arms. I used one of my recently deceased grandfather's canes to hook the toys and pull them toward me when I needed them. One day, Pop Ryan's cane came up in conversation.

"Why are you keeping Pop's old cane?"

"I miss him and the cane reminds me of him."

Favoring a smaller keepsake, Mom said, "Why don't you take a couple of my old photographs of Pop and keep them in your wallet?"

"It's not the same," I said. "He owned this!"

Mom's eyes softened and she gave me a hug.

Fibbing is a fair weapon when dealing with a cold, cunning opponent.

Midnight Harmony

*Mom, Dad, Rory, and I sing softly together
in the small, dark bedroom. The hum of our
only air-conditioner is the sole accompaniment.*

August 1966: It was midnight, and the heat had created a
film of sweat between my underwear and me. I couldn't take
it. I dragged my mattress through the narrow doorway and—
"POW!"—my knuckles rapped the wall.

"Ouch!"

"Be quiet!" Dad yelled. I ignored his weak attempt to
keep me in my hot stinky room.

With the mattress pulled around me, I squeezed through
the doorway to my parents' bedroom, easing the sheet aside.

**All together,
83rd Street
corner, 1957.**

The sheet was tacked over the doorway because there was no door. One of Dad's innovations. My father's ongoing grunts and moans drowned out the other sound in the room, the hum of the apartment's single air conditioner. I scanned the room's perimeter for a sleeping spot. Rory had arrived in the bedroom earlier, dropping himself alongside my parents' bed, his mattress curled up like Canadian bacon in the small space between the bed and the wall. This left me no option but to lay my mattress perpendicular over the bottom of his.

Once my mattress was in place, we were four bugs in a rug, and the curtain rose on a summer play. Rory bellowed from way low in his belly, "Good night, Momma. Good night, Dada. And good night, Thommmmm."

I answered lower—limbo low. "Good nigh', Ma, good nigh', Da, and good nigh', Rorio." Then I went high as Bugs Bunny to Elmer Fudd. "Rorio, Rorio, wherefore art thou, Rorio?"

Dad said, "Everyone shut up or get back in your bedroom. Go to sleep!"

A moment passed. Nothing happened. Then another moment. Again nothing. After a bit of time, a slow, steady "Whistle While You Work" rose from the ashes of the silence. It gained momentum and then Mom entered the studio to step up to the mike. A trio was now in song, in tune, and in danger, depending on Dad. He was a lion in a cave with a thorn in his paw and the scene had the potential for a not-happy ending. It was dark, but not too dark. We all continued to whistle and watch Dad squirm under his covers. He was a plutonium heap. Fusion might be imminent.

Continuing to whistle while we worked, Mom, Rory, and I seamlessly moved into another tune, singing loud and proud:

"Pack up your troubles in your old kit bag
And smile, smile, smile!"

As the song hit its second verse, Dad's anger was softened by sweet nostalgia and we began our sentimental journey.

Telling Dad what to do with his camera.

World War I tunes, World War II tunes—give him a war and Dad gave you a tune.

Civil War? "When Johnny Comes Marching Home." Revolutionary War? "Yankee Doodle." Crimean War? OK, no song there, but you could see his eyes calculating and searching his deep memory. Nothing like a good tune from a good war to calm the beast until he lies down with the lamb.

As a child I thought Warner Brothers was the government. Its films played around the clock on our TV. Nothing intoxicated Dad like a nostalgic trip through film land, especially a flick that included grey battleships rolling over the cold Atlantic waves. He favored the European theater over the Pacific. *The World at War* TV documentary series made Dad snap to attention when its theme music began. To counter Dad's anger, Rory and I would sometimes dip into our bag of nostalgia tricks. They were all powerful, but most potent if used with reasonable caution and only when needed.

In song that summer night, we soared and dove through the dark, chilled bedroom, all together as a family like we were at no other time, unless you count fighting over the last slice of bacon. Our song rolled to a happy conclusion when all the lines were lost to exhaustion except *"Pack up your troubles in your old kit bag and smile, smile, smile."* The four of us, twin Laurel and Hardy's, skipped arm in arm out of the last scene, as the credits began rolling across our dusty pants.

Graveyard Cough

It's just a slight clearing of my throat,
but to Dad's ears it's the death rattle
of his tuberculosis-afflicted father.

I'm 12. It's right after dinner on a school night in early December 1966. I'm in the living room, and I clear my throat a little.

"Get another sweatshirt!"

"Oh, crap," I thought, and grabbed more clothes and presented myself for my father's review.

He counted my garments and said, "OK, be back by nine."

Dad and I were at war. All my life, if I got the slightest cold, a little tickle in my throat, it turned into a graveyard cough. In his mind's eye, it would start in my feet, travel through every chamber in my pulmonary system, and build in pressure and size until it burst out of my mouth like the death rattle of a tuberculosis victim who was simultaneously taking a series of bullets to his lungs. If Dad heard my tiny cough two rooms away he'd ambush me and sandwich me with two T-shirts, two of his old sweatshirts and a giant jar of Vick's VapoRub. He put three fingers in the jar, take out enough yuck to cure a choir of sore throats, and rub it into my chest and neck like I owed him a lot of money.

My Dad's dad, Thomas E. Pryor, died at age 40. He had advanced tuberculosis. They called it Pott's Disease. Whenever I coughed my Dad probably saw pictures of the sanatorium where my grandfather spent seven of his last ten years, a hundred miles upstate.

On my way down the stairs I started undressing. By the time I got to the first floor I was down to a T-shirt and a light sweatshirt, optimal clothing for touch football. I put my extra sweatshirt, my peacoat, and my scarf behind the radia-

**Mom giving
Dad the
business.**

tor near the cellar door and left the vestibule. Jumping off my stoop, I looked up at the snowflakes dancing across the streetlights and followed their wavy paths down until they dusted the street. Then I wandered over to First Avenue to meet my friends.

After two hours and three games, it was time to go home— and it was time to pee. Running into the hallway and up the stairs, determined to get to the toilet fast, I forgot the outerwear I had hidden in the vestibule. I ran into the bathroom, passed my mother doing the dishes, and relieved myself in a religious ritual. Finished, clueless, I stepped out of the bathroom into the kitchen at the same time my Dad stepped into the kitchen from the living room. He looked me over.

"Did you just get in?"

My mouth wide open, I said nothing, once again having entered the land of unanswerable questions.

"I said, 'Did you just...' " Mom cut Dad off.

"Are you friggin' nuts? He's been home ten minutes in his room. If you paid any deeper attention to *The World at War* on TV you could go right into the sea battle."

Dad was ready to say something, but shrugged and went back into the living room. The commercial was over and it was time for him to return to the North Atlantic in 1942.

Mom said loud enough for Dad to hear, "Tommy, here's a dollar, go get two milk." She pushed me out the door with the buck before Dad came back in the room. Even with the door closed, from the hall stairs I heard him say to Mom, "We have three quarts, what the hell is wrong with you?"

"Don't have a conniption. You all drink milk like this is a farm. It will be gone tomorrow, I'm not your Gunga Din. Tommy's on an exercise kick. I'm helping him out."

I ran down the stairs with a shit-ass grin, in love with Mom all over again.

Cowboys to Girls

1967–1972

The Holy Cart

*The St. Anthony statuettes
are selling like hotcakes, Sister Mercedes!*

"It's not going to happen."

"Please, Dad!"

"One record player is enough for this house."

"You never let me near it."

"I don't trust you."

"I'm your son."

"You're clumsy."

Dad has squashed my request to borrow money to buy Joe Skrapits's portable record player.

Joe had said, "If you come up with $35 before the Christmas break, I'll sell you the Phillips."

It was late October. The record player was beautiful. I had two months and six dollars. All my friends were officially broke. Mom only had her house money and that barely made it through the week. She couldn't help me. I needed a plan.

The parish needed money all the time. It ran fifty/fifty clubs, cake sales, bingo. The low earner was the religious article store in the rear of the church. The store, which sold crucifixes, religious statues, and catechisms, was a flop. Kids never went in. Mrs. Hutzpacker, who ran the place, was mostly deaf, six feet tall, and looked like Boris Karloff. She'd come up to your face and yell, "I CAN'T HEAR YOU. SPEAK UP." Whether you had said anything or not.

This sluggish business smelled like an opportunity to me. I approached my eighth-grade teacher, Sister Mercedes.

"Sister, do you know the religious article store is going down the tubes?"

She gave me a funny look, but I kept talking.

"If kids won't go to the store, let's bring the store to the kids. I'll go around to each classroom on Friday selling re-

Shadow of St. Stephen's steeple.

ligious articles and do my best to separate weekend money from each kid's pocket."

I watched the nun's expression. Her lips pulled to one side of her face and her eyes narrowed. Her finger stroking her chin meant that I had a pilot program. She knew I had years of business experience selling milk and toast during morning recess. Besides, the priests and nuns were united on only one thing: anything other than illegal drug sales was a legitimate way to raise money for St. Stephen's.

I started slow, selling a few catechisms and rosary beads. The first two weeks, I made only two dollars. I worried that I'd never have my own record player. (Sister Mercedes worked out a deal for me to receive 5 percent of all my sales).

Joe Skrapits, the same kid who was selling the record player, approached me in the schoolyard at lunch one day.

"Hey Pryor, do you have a St. Anthony statue for sale?"

"No, why?"

"St. Anthony is the patron saint for finding lost articles, stupid. My father's always losing things and cursing around the house. Mom says she's had it, and she's leaving all of us unless Dad stops his ranting and raving. Mom's a great cook, Dad can't cook—and I love to eat!"

Normally, I would've been hurt by his calling me stupid. Not that time. I replied, "Joe, I'll fill your order next Friday."

I grabbed my milk box and ran out of the yard. I had discovered my secret weapon—the Catholic Church roster of saints, a lineup more powerful than the 1961 Yankees. Joe Skrapits would get his St. Anthony statue next Friday, and I'd spend my week researching everyone's birthday. Each day of the year, the Catholic Church celebrates a martyr or other saint. My plan was to get every kid to buy a statue of the saint who shares his special day.

I didn't stop with birthdays. Every profession also has a patron saint or angel. The next Friday, I sold three Michael the Archangel statues to kids whose dads were cops. Attila Krupincza bought a St. Vincent statue for his grandfather, a plumber. I sold a St. Julian to Marianne Stranklee, whose uncle was in a Hungarian circus. St. Julian is the patron saint of jugglers. Steve Gabriel had four cats, a parakeet and a turtle. Steve purchased a St. Francis of Assisi.

"Unlike Doctor Doolittle," I told Steve, "St. Francis really did talk to the animals."

Donald Matthews was always getting into trouble with the nuns, his parents, everybody. Plus, he had a wicked neck twitch. I gave him a St. Jude statue as a personal gift.

"Here Donald, put this in your pocket and keep it there."

"Why?"

"Just do it. Trust me."

I didn't have the heart to tell him that St. Jude is the patron saint of hopeless cases.

With this sudden burst in sales, I needed to expand my operation. Sister Mercedes, now functioning as my business manager, borrowed a metal two-shelf cart from "Mom," the school lunch lady. I knelt on one knee and said, "I dub thee the Holy Cart."

Traveling the school's halls, I reminded everyone to save their pennies for Friday, when the Holy Cart rolled into town with gifts and notions for every occasion. I assured my fellow altar boys that the Holy Ghost loved making sales calls with me.

"Each Friday, he leaves his perch on the side of the altar to fly alongside the Holy Cart on its rounds. We're a liturgical team!"

My colleagues made circles around the sides of their heads while whistling.

Father Edward heard about my venture and decided we should have a talk. "Thomas, you need to promote the Church when you visit the classrooms," he said. "Say things to get the children excited about religion."

Good suggestion—I borrowed a thick book from the nuns' library titled The *Lives and Deaths of 1000 Saints*. Great stuff. Gory murders, disembowelments, stone crushings, more methods for dying violently then I ever imagined. It was a quick read.

Armed with this knowledge, I developed a routine for my Holy Cart visits. Every week, I brought three "Fun Facts About the Saints" with me. I'd try to mix it up, one famous saint, one obscure saint, and a third saint who had had an extremely bad day.

Sometimes, I'd pick a bizarre one. "Wulfstan was smitten by a fair young lady at a village dance," I'd say. "To distract himself from the impure thoughts running through his head, Wulfstan threw himself into a nearby thicket of thorn bushes. He stayed there until the impure thoughts painfully passed away. God was so impressed by the saint's efforts that he prevented Wulfstan from ever having those feelings again."

I closed the book with a clap and said, "Isn't that great, kids?"

All ears perked up for that one. Sister Mercedes seemed edgy during the telling.

By my last week, I still needed a miracle to get my record player. I tried hard not to spend my money on other things, but I was still eleven dollars short. That Friday, I woke early, checked my inventory, and headed off to knock on some classroom doors. My best seller was a plastic statue of Mary in an alcove appearing to the faithful. The alcove looked like a miniature missile silo, with two pieces meeting in the front like a curtain. You slid the pieces apart to reveal Mary inside a grotto with open arms standing on a rock. The problem was that the alcove was long and thin and so, too, was Mary long and thin—real long and catwalk thin.

The quirky product had sold well, but I knew it could sell even better. I put my sales skills to work, and when I stepped in front of the class I had a plan.

"Folks, I have something special for you today. Something the Church has hidden for years, but now proudly presents to you for the first time."

I turned away from the kids, picked up the statue, and spun back to the class, opening the alcove doors.

"I give you Skinny Mary, Pre-pregnancy Mary, the Mary with a twinkle in her eye and a song in her heart."

The class took a deep breath, and then exploded. Based on normal nun behavior, I expected to be wrestled to the ground like a Presidential assassin. It didn't happen. Sister Mercedes stood to the side, covering her mouth but not enough to completely hide the fact that she was laughing.

I made three dollars that last day, with sales that included six skinny Marys at 75 cents apiece. I had $27 total. Not enough. Joe Skrapits was leaving for his grandparents' in the morning and taking his suitcase-shaped record player with him. I dragged myself home. Mom met me at the door. "Why the puss?"

"I'm shy eight dollars."

"Honey, I wish I could, I truly wish I could."

"I know," I said. I dropped my stuff and left for the park.

At dinnertime, I walked into the apartment. Mom was facing the stove, stirring the Italian sauce. She didn't turn around to say hello to me. Weird.

Then she told me, "Go in your room until supper's ready." Double weird.

I went to my room. Taking the crap out of my pocket, I noticed something stuck under my Mickey Mantle bobblehead doll. It was eight crumpled singles.

Five minutes later, Dad walked through the door, Rory came into the kitchen and the four of us sat down to eat. Dad grabbed the sauce bowl and gave it a look-over.

"Where's the sausage? Where's the meatballs?"

"Ah jeez, I forgot the meat again," Mom answered. Then she turned to me and said, "Tommy, how'd it go today?"

"Good Mom, really good. I made my mark."

Dad dropped his fork. Mom gave me a smile. Dad gave Mom the look. Rory grinned. We were going to have music in our room.

Indoor Tackle

Mr. and Mrs. Murphy never caught us playing football in their apartment. But once at dinner, Mr. Murphy did wonder why his home smelled like a gym.

In 1963, a twenty-story building with modern floor plans went up around the corner from my house. Suddenly, I had friends who lived in apartments with huge living rooms—perfect spaces for indoor tackle. We targeted the three-bedroom units with working parents and latchkey kids.

"Help me with the TV," Steve Murphy said one day. His family lived in one of those apartments, on the second floor. He was holding one end of his family's six-foot-long TV console in mid-air.

Readying my helmet, Our Lady
of Good Counsel Rams, 1968.

I rushed to get the other end.

"Dad says it's the best piece of furniture he's ever owned," Steve said. "He calls it exquisite Italianate wood, so go slow and easy. Jesus H. Christ, watch the walls!"

Steve's two brothers moved the lamps and side tables into the bedroom and stood the couch and love seat up on their ends in the galley kitchen.

"The big lamp nearly hit the light fixture," Steve warned. "Be careful when we move it back." Then the doorbell rang and we froze, thinking it was Steve's parents. I opened the door slowly, and Artie and Jamie Peters bounded in.

"When's kickoff?" Artie said.

The Murphy living room was harsh turf; there was no rug, only cold linoleum glued to a concrete floor. It was as hard as Lambeau Field, the tundra home of the Green Bay Packers. Everyone wore elbow and knee pads. We kept the windows wide open to lessen the chance of breaking one. It was no big deal if the ball sailed through the window; in fact it was beautiful to watch the spiraling ball taking a clean sweet ride. To retrieve it, we'd hang from the windowsill, plant our feet on the ledge halfway down, and slip down to the street. It was just another play.

The Murphy parents never got home before six, a clockwork schedule that kept the game going. (At the dinner table one time, though, Mr. Murphy made a face and said, "Jesus, Mary and Joseph, this house smells like a gymnasium.")

Still, we craved a bone-friendly surface. Blacks and blues covered our bodies. The Peters boys offered an alternative. Artie and Jamie lived upstairs on the seventh floor—same layout —except they had carpeting. Mr. Peters, their father, was a garbage man. He looked like the generously proportioned actor, William Conrad, who played the detective on TV's *Cannon*. One day he heard us gabbing about our game downstairs and leaned into our conversation.

"You play tackle in Murphy's?"

I was shell-shocked, but Artie and Jamie knew their father.

"As much as we can," Artie said.

"Does the old man know?" Mr. Peters asked.

Jamie laughed so hard, soda passed through his nose.

"Are you kidding?" Artie said.

"Do you want to play here? Wall-to-wall carpeting?" Mr. Peters asked, arching his thick eyebrows up and down.

"Absolutely," I said.

Artie and Jamie shot me a look. Artie said to his father, "What about Mom?"

"Mmmm… Yes, the Missus. The Missus? The Missus will be a problem." He drummed a finger on the cleft of his chin. "She hits the stores on Saturday—hairdresser, Woolworth's, Schaller & Weber, the A&P, and the Chinese laundry. She's gone at least three hours, sometimes four. I guarantee three hours. I'll referee. We'll put the entertainment center face down on my bed. We'll move the breakfront to the hall, couches to the galley kitchen, and the rest of the stuff we can swing into the bedrooms."

Mr. Peters was on a roll.

"Everyone wears socks with no shoes, no sneakers. You all wear gloves to minimize scuffing the walls."

"Dad, you're getting carried away," Artie said. "We don't need gloves."

"She'll catch the marks on the wall before she steps through the door," Mr. Peters answered. "We'll be dead."

"No, with gloves we won't be able to catch the ball," Artie answered. "We'll hang bedsheets on the walls with masking tape."

Mr. Peters smiled proudly. "That's my boy."

I was in *The Twilight Zone*. A dad was planning indoor fireworks while plotting to outwit a tough, doesn't-miss-a-thing mother. My father tried to outwit my mother every day, but that was on his own behalf. His polished lying and conniving were not available for rent. I'd never heard of an inside job, where one parent helped the kids fake out the other parent.

For two months all went well. Then, one Saturday, in the middle of a goal-line stand, the front door burst open. Mrs.

Peters was back early. Mr. Peters, in shock, forgot to whistle the play dead. Behind my block, Jamie picked up the needed yards on a right-end sweep. He dove over two defenders, passing within inches of his mother's head. After ducking Jamie's body, Mrs. Peters assumed a drill sergeant stance and screamed at Mr. Peters until his arms hung slack at his sides. The beating was brutal and a double loss because big-mouth Steve Murphy had told his parents about our game in his place after we had moved it to the Peters apartment. Now we had no field at all.

Mulling it over, we sat on parked cars in the street, discussing the difference between wall-to-wall carpet and linoleum surfaces. We realized that, despite the assortment of injuries that we suffered on the Murphy's field, no one had ever broken a bone.

"What's the difference between linoleum and sidewalk concrete?" Steve said, continuing the analysis.

"Let me cut a sample from each and smack you in the head," Artie said.

Steve shook Artie off. "Really, if we load up on sweatshirts, put a few pairs of shorts over our dungarees and wear pads, do you think it's any worse than the linoleum?"

This was seamless logic, I thought. Everyone grumbled, but eventually agreed. Steve's schemes always seemed good going in.

Our new field was York Avenue from 81st Street to 82nd Street. Everything on the sidewalk was in bounds: fire hydrants, trees, phone booths, mailboxes, light poles, signs, meters, and pedestrians. We did our best to accommodate people, giving folks walk-around-us room, but if the game was tight, we'd use a lady carrying a few brown bags as a blocker. At some point in each game, the inanimate objects attached to the sidewalk joined in.

"Oh, crap, I hit my head, time-out, time-out—Cupo, you're an asshole," Steve would scream after being shoved into a streetlight.

Time-outs were my favorite part of the game. When one was called, everybody had to freeze in position so we could take an imaginary picture and remember all players' exact locations. Then we'd check out the injured party or let a guy retie his sneakers. Once we were set, everyone had to resume their frozen pose. The lying and cheating over these locations was great street opera. No one gave in.

"I was here."

"No, you were there."

"I was *here!*"

"No, you were *there!*"

Play restarted. Arguments were settled by getting even.

Four years later, in 1967, the neighborhood parishes formed a tackle football league for boys 13 and up. Our sidewalk games faded away.

Dad's Promise

Dad finally makes good on his pledge to get me to a Giants football game. My ticket is another guy's hangover.

I was a fanatic for the football Giants, with an indelible lowercase "ny" scratched onto the wall of my heart. But, tickets were scarce for home games at Yankee Stadium, so although they needed my support I couldn't get there to give it to them.

My frustration was bursting. I would beg Dad to take me, but all pleas met the same answer.

"Hon, I'm sorry. When you're older, I promise."

Fast forward a few years. I was playing football for the Our Lady of Good Counsel Rams, the local church team, and our home field was the dust bowl just inside Central Park on 97th Street off Fifth Avenue. Dad never missed a game and came to many of my practices. Walking home along Madison Avenue from the dust bowl one day in 1967, we talked.

"Dad, will I ever get to a Giants home game?"

He delayed answering. "How's the subway been?"

"Not bad."

I had just started riding the subway alone that past year (at least as far as he knew).

"You know five Loftus regulars have season tickets and they keep the tickets under the bar's register," Dad said. "And you know that these guys spend a lot of time in the bar."

Of course I knew. I could walk into Loftus Tavern blindfolded, go to the back of the bar and put a dime in the jukebox without making contact with a stool, wall, or table. Dad was such a regular himself, he could have taken his mail there. I nodded.

He continued, "Well, sometimes one of those guys doesn't feel too well on Sunday morning, and Jack Loftus gets a call. Then somebody else gets a call, and that person gets to go to the game."

Loftus Tavern, 1962.

"Since you're on the subway now, maybe you could work this for yourself," Dad suggested.

My head felt like it was exploding. "How?"

"Go down to the bar around eleven on Sunday. Jack keeps the place locked until noon, but you'll see him in the back, drinking coffee and reading the paper. Tap on the back door window. He'll let you in. See what happens."

The next Sunday the Giants were playing the Saints at home. At eleven sharp, I tapped on the tavern window. Jack took his reading glasses off, saw me and came to the door.

"Good morning, Tommy. How are you?"

"Fine, Jack, just great."

"What can I do for you?"

"Could I come in?"

"Well, the cops will have my license if I serve you a drink before twelve, but a Coke won't harm anybody."

He winked and let me in, locking the door behind us. I hopped on a stool and made a bridge with my ten fingers. Jack dropped two maraschino cherries in my glass.

"Jack, were all the guys here last night?"

"What guys?"

"The guys who go to the game with you?"

"Yes, everyone made an appearance. Chris and Orson were the last two out the door."

"Did either of them look sick or anything?"

"Well, neither one looks that good to start with, but Orson, he made a couple of passes at the coatrack on his way out."

I wiped my face with my hand and opened the newspaper. The phone rang. I nearly fell backwards off the stool. I crossed my fingers under the bar.

"Hello Mikey, how are you?"

I relaxed. It was Jack's brother. He had season tickets, too. He owned a bar in Sunnyside, Queens.

Jack hung up, saw my face and said, "Cheer up, lad. It's only 11:30. Game starts at 1:35. There's still plenty of time."

Jack knew why I was there. Dad and Jack were in cahoots.

At five to twelve, the phone rang again. I held my breath.

"Oh, Orson, I'm sorry to hear that. You seemed a wee down last night. Probably the flu. Tommy Pryor's here, do you mind if I give him your ticket?"

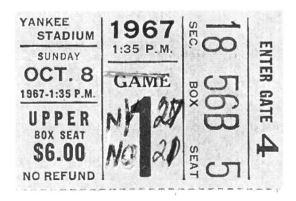

My heart was ripping a hole through my chest. Jack hung the phone up and slid his gigantic hand under the register, pulling out five red tickets, and held them up like a winning hand of cards.

"Here it is…seat number 5…you're right next to me. Do you want to wait for the other guys and we'll pile into a Checker together?"

"No, Jack, I want to get up there and sit in the crowd as the place fills up. Thanks so much."

I shook his hand and flew out the door toward the 86th Street subway station. Twenty-five minutes later, I was in my seat at Yankee Stadium.

I memorized the ticket stub. Mezzanine, Section 18, Box 56B, Seat 5. I looked down on the field and saw Joe Morrison wearing his pregame Yankee cap, Ernie Koy, Tucker Fredrickson, and Spider Lockhart, all warming up. They were my favorite players. I was home. Dad kept his promise.

Allie and Rory in boxing pose.

The Playtex Chapel

We carry the stewardesses' wash, they feed us hot chocolate, and then in their bathroom I see four white bras. I quickly silence that pesky little voice in my ear.

"My turn," Steve Murphy said. We switched positions. My fingers were so cold I could've snapped them off. As we threw the football in front of the Laundromat on York Avenue, the store's exhaust fan blasted hot air onto the frozen sidewalk. Every three minutes, Steve and I traded locations, planting one of us directly under the delicious steam.

Even at 13 degrees, gloves were forbidden. The leather football was expensive, the sidewalk was concrete, and the street was asphalt. Dropping the ball was a criminal offense. Steve and I practically gave up playing all other sports. Year round, one of us carried a football. We took every opportunity to improve our catching skills. We were indentured servants to two older boys. They were the quarterbacks, we were their catch robots, and practice was mandatory.

The single thing that interrupted our concentration was a pretty girl. Our standards were high. Steve and I were 12 years old, experienced connoisseurs—we didn't slow our game down for just any girl. And really, that's all that happened, our game slowed down. When an attractive girl walked by, we'd each give her a sturdy look. If we didn't drop the ball, we'd exchange small nods acknowledging that we were impressed with each other's ability to do two equally important things at the same time.

The only time our game came to a halt was for two Air Canada stewardesses, Marie and Justine. They were stationed in New York on rotation. Every ten days or so, they'd do their wash in the Laundromat. Their stunning beauty, two Playboy bunnies with wings, broke up our game. Oh my God! Marie, tall and beautiful, Justine, taller and beauti-

Steve Murphy, a charmer even when delivering dry cleaning, 1969.

ful. Every time we saw them coming down the block we'd act like two kittens hearing the can opener working a tin of "Seafood Feast." We'd stop our catch and hold our hands up like traffic cops, signaling to the stewardesses that it was safe to pass. They smiled at us going into and coming out of the store. Each of their smiles was a body blow, a slight heart attack that sent blood racing to our faces and struck our teeth into frozen grins. I fantasized about asking them if we could carry their wash, but I never worked up the guts to do that. Steve, brave and handsome, took his shot as they came out of the store one day with their collars turned up. They looked so cute that way.

"Excuse me, Miss. Can we carry your wash?"

They looked at each other, shrugged, and said, "Oui," then turned the bags over to us. I thank the Lord every day for allowing me to stand in Steve's shadow. He was a girl magnet. I put the football in my bag and slung it over my shoulder.

We strutted down the street—two sailors coming home to our best girls after a year at sea. Stopping at their building, they thanked us and tried to take the bags away. I cradled mine the way a mother holds her sickly child.

Steve blurted, "No, no, they're too heavy. Let us take them up the stairs."

The girls, too cold to argue, let us keep the bags, and we all climbed the five flights to their apartment. Inside the door Marie kicked off her heels and said, "*J'ai très mal aux pieds.*"

Justine translated for us, "Her feet are killing her."

"Boys, merci, merci…put zee bags on floor," said Marie.

"Want some sing to drink?" offered Justine.

"No, thanks," said Steve. I elbowed him in the ribs.

"How about some hot chocolate?" I said, rubbing my hands together. I looked more pathetic than Jackie Cooper when he played the son of a drunken boxer in *The Champ*.

"Do we have un chocolat chaud?" Marie asked.

"*Mais oui,*" said Justine.

The ladies exchanged an "OK, but that's it" look.

Steve and I exchanged our own look: "Is this great or what?"

We sat down, taking off our Navy peacoats, each shy a few buttons. Justine prepared the hot chocolate and our eyes flew around the apartment. We were in heaven and wanted to remember the layout. I asked to use the bathroom.

Once in there, I saw something that made me freeze mid-pee. Hanging from the shower curtain rod were four bras. Stunned, I stood on the tub's edge to get a better look. The bras looked like the dead cardinal hats that hang from the ceiling rafters in St. Patrick's Cathedral. I dismissed the little altar boy voice in my ear telling me, "Get down, and be good." The bras were beautiful. The bras were white and their tags said Playtex. I touched them. I smelled them. I kissed them. I would have licked them, but when I kissed them they tasted like soap. I was hoping for girls' boob taste—whatever that was. After a thorough investigation of every stitch on every bra, I returned to the kitchen.

"Steve, I'm done, you can go to the bathroom now."

"I don't have to go."

I buried my best look in Steve's eyes.

"Steve, you really should go. We're going back outside and you'll only have to go later on."

My eyebrows worked furiously and my head tilted toward the "Hall of Bras." Aggravated, he said, "But I don't have..."

"Ouch."

Looking back at me strangely, Steve limped to the bathroom. After an equally long time, Steve returned to the table with a glazed look usually reserved for seeing the face of God. Our hot chocolates went cold. The ladies reheated them. We talked; Marie and Justine were both from Montreal. They'd been working for Air Canada for two years and they loved traveling and meeting new and different people. They split the New York apartment with two other stewardesses who had alternate schedules. Their perfume tickled my nose. I think it was Cachet. I drifted away...

Marie was Miss December. Curly black hair, dark brown eyes—two Hershey kisses. She was tall and athletic. She moved the kitchen chairs around with one arm. I saw her muscles through her sheer blouse. Her dream was to own a horse farm one day. She was a centerfold and there were no staples to keep her locked inside the magazine. Her lips were perfect—pink with a trace of wetness. She made an audible pop with her lips.

Justine was Miss January, with her long blonde hair and eyes of blue. She planned to join the Peace Corps to help those who couldn't help themselves. Justine loved relaxing at home in a man's tailored shirt. Her eyebrows were light brown wisps, one higher than the other in the resting position. They made her look frisky: "And what do you have in mind?" Her cheeks were rosy and chubby cute—ready to store nuts for the winter. Her mouth was smaller than Marie's. It made a perfect "O" when she enjoyed something we said. I was addicted to the "O" and worked hard to come up with clever statements to invite it out as often as possible. If the "O" had a hand, I would've held it.

Focusing on the girls' voices, I became aware that my ear was an instrument of pleasure. Each time one of them spoke, a French accent sailed through the air. Sometimes a single French word or short phrase posed as a whole song:

"Au revoir." "Savoir-faire." "Adieu."

Each syllable headed for my heart, waking up a gang of monkeys who drove a truck into my stomach where they did cartwheels and headstands. I tried looking thoughtful about whatever the girls said. I'd pretend I understood, but I barely registered a word. The siren melody took me away.

After the fastest hour in my life, Marie said, *"On a sommeil.* It is time to sleep. *Desolée,* you must go now."

"Desolée." I whispered the word over my tongue and around my mouth.

We both said *"Bon voyage"* on the way out. Steve and I punched and tackled our way down the five flights of stairs until we landed in a heap on the ground floor. Laughing our heads off, we repeated two words over and over again. "C cups, C cups, C cups..."

The next two weeks crawled. For the first time in my life, I voluntarily went to bed early to get the night over with as soon as possible.

Around the time we expected the girls to return to New York, we stood guard in front of the Laundromat. Every night we packed food into our pockets to stave off hunger. Passing time, we counted our tosses. On the third night of our watch, I dropped the ball when I spied the girls coming up the block. We ran down to meet them and took their bags.

"How are you? Did the passengers treat you right?" we asked.

They laughed and said, *"Très bien."*

We knew that meant fine. We had borrowed Steve's mother's French/English translation dictionary.

From that point on, the visit's routine was the same with one exception—we went to the bathroom twice, now that we were devoted parishioners of the Playtex Chapel. While they made hot chocolate, they asked us, "You like rock and roll and hockey?" What a question!

"Yes! Why?"

"*Mon père* is an NBC executive," Marie said. "You know zee TV music show *Hullabaloo*? He maybe get us tickets."

While we chewed on that, Justine told us that Reggie Fleming, a star player for the New York Rangers, was her friend. This news electrified us.

"Do you prefer *Hullabaloo* or a Ranger game?" they asked.

Steve and I said in unison, "Why can't we do both?"

They said, "*Magnifique!*"

We all smiled.

Marie said, "Next time in New York, we go to *Hullabaloo*. Give me your phone numbers. I call you."

Our plans, which now included stewardesses, Madison Square Garden, and a TV show, left our parents puzzled, worried, and/or indifferent, depending on when it came up. I don't think they believed us. Any repeated mention of the subject within earshot of my parents triggered a headshake, a face twitch or a deep, dumb stare. Each night I parked myself in front of the telephone until I was forced into bed.

"First you're going to bed early, now you're passing out with your hand over the phone," Mom said as she dragged me down the hall. "Are you a prison warden expecting a call from the Governor's office?"

After too many nights, Marie called.

"It eez set. We go to *Hullabaloo* at NBC studios in Brooklyn, February 21. The show's hosts are zee Righteous Brothers—eez a tribute to zee Beatles' *Rubber Soul*."

I said nothing. I was numb.

"Tom? *Bonjour*, hello, Tom, are you there?" Marie said.

"Yes."

"Good. The guests are Paul Revere, Bob Lind, and Nancy Sinatra. I hear sheez bringing her walking boots."

The night of the show, we piled into a Checker cab. Though it had those pull-up seats on the floor that we loved to bounce on, Steve and I squeezed in between the girls. This was my first time over the Brooklyn Bridge. The New York skyline was stunning in the clear winter air, but my five senses were focused on the girls. I timed their breathing and joined its rhythm. Every bump in the road made me collide with Justine. I measured every one of her curves. It was remarkable how many ins and outs she had.

When we arrived at the studio the show was delayed. We waited on line. The icy wind howled. Steve and I were thoroughly eau de cologned with "Old Spice" aftershave and wore our drafty peacoats. We had on dress shirts with no sweaters because we couldn't hide our best shirts from our best girls. We froze. The girls had on full-length fur coats, and they saw the shape we were in. They whispered to each other, turned to us, and said, "Are you cold?" We nodded yes, like trick horses in a carnival. They opened their coats and said, "Come in."

Now, you'd think we would've jumped straight into their open arms. But it wasn't like that. Nope, it didn't happen that way at all. Steve and I made full eye contact. Memorializing the event came first. Only then did we move toward the two heartbreakers. We had to stretch it out. We knew it would never happen again.

During the show, the Righteous Brothers did a medley of songs from *Rubber Soul.* I had my eyes on Justine. She was singing along and her mouth formed that perfect "O." My toughest decision all night was, Do I watch Marie, Justine, or the singers? My neck and my heart got a workout.

Later that month, the girls took us to two Ranger hockey games. At each game, Reggie Fleming came off the ice during warm-ups to greet us. He gave Steve and me Ranger media guides that were not available to the public. Reggie rubbed our crew cuts. This news made us neighborhood gods; you couldn't miss us, it was like we were eight months pregnant.

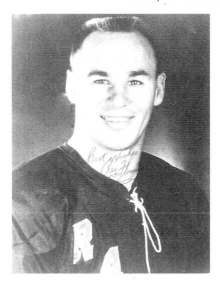

At the beginning of March, the girls were late getting back to New York. We kept vigil in front of the Laundromat each night, rain, hail, or snow. But no girls. Mid-month, we sat on their stoop to see if we could figure out who their other two roommates were and ask them what happened to Marie and Justine. The second night, a very pretty woman came up the stoop with a bag of groceries.

"Excuse me, Miss, do you know Marie or Justine?"

"*Oui.*"

"Where are they?"

"Are you the two boys who carried their wash?"

"Yes. What happened to them?"

"They were reassigned and will no longer be in New York. They told us that they felt very bad that they could not say goodbye to you."

Our hearts fell to our feet. The woman went into the lobby. We said nothing. It was over.

Steve and I walked up the street to the Laundromat and began throwing the football hard at each other. Good strong throws with mustard on them. The kind of passes that opened my chest up, rang my arm out, and hurt my hands when I caught it. It felt good. It felt good to feel something, because I wasn't sure the numbness would ever go away. But getting back to catch was headed in the right direction and the ball flew sweetly. A tall young woman with a load of wash slid past Steve and me. We both gave her the eye and didn't drop the ball. When she passed through the Laundromat door, Steve and I exchanged a sturdy look. It was getting warmer.

Kenny Devoe's Magical Nose

Sometimes, altar boys carry huge candles during church rituals. For Kenny, this is problematic.

Walking to school the day Mom asked Dad for a house money raise, I smiled. I had remembered that it was Good Friday, and that meant we'd be doing the Stations of the Cross in the church that afternoon. Right after lunch, I said, "Sister, can I be excused?" The nun made a face, but she had to let me go down to the sacristy to transform into an altar boy. The rest of the class and the whole school assembled in the pews a half hour later.

Kids ate up the Stations of the Cross. It was theater. Two altar boys with gigantic candles would stand to the side of a third altar boy carrying Jesus on what looked like a heavy duty stickball bat with a crucifix on top. You felt like you were in the Roman Legion and you got to leave the altar to walk up and down the church aisles—"Look at me!" You would stand right next to your chums and some very pretty older girls who couldn't make you go away.

That afternoon things got interesting.

Kenny Devoe, one of the altar boys, loved altar wine, but, for some reason, would never drink it directly from the gallon jug. He carefully poured the wine into the cruet, the tiny glass vessel that was used during the Mass. This drove me crazy. First there was the problem of a 12-year-old drinking wine. But second, did Kenny think he was going to get into more trouble or less trouble based on his method for drinking it? His slow wine transfer meant that his chances of getting caught were sky high. And, if Kenny got busted, our indictments were sealed. The school rule? If you were there, you did it.

That day, Kenny drank too much. When the altar bells rang, we walked out of the sacristy with the priest to start the

Kenny Devoe at LaSalle, 1969.

procession. I had a candle, Smithy had the cross, and Kenny had the other candle. At the ninth station, when Jesus falls for the third time while carrying the cross, the entire student body cheers him on with the practiced sarcasm we learned from first grade onward. They read from their missals: "Jesus—exhausted—in pain—for the third and final time!" Long pause here. "BUT, NO! Jesus rose and struggled on!"

Three hundred little boxing announcers sounding like Don Dunphy at ringside were screaming, "Our Lord has risen from the canvas and is back in the heat of the battle!" The nuns flew around the church wanting to thump somebody, but really couldn't do anything while the insolent children picked up their reading speed—now aiming for early dismissal. The nuns tried to slow it down, but to no avail.

After a good giggle, I looked around the church for some of my friends when I noticed Kenny was nodding off into the flame at the top of his candle. I nudged Smithy, who nudged Kenny, but Kenny was well past the point. He was a sleeping horse standing up in his stall. After a harder nudge from Smithy, Kenny lifted up his head with a jolt and wiggled his nose. Then he gradually dropped back into the flame.

We pulled Kenny along through the rest of the stations, but by the end, his nose smelled like skirt steak. Kenny left the altar boys that week. His nose, first purple, and then red for a year, became Kenny Devoe's Magical Nose.

A Valentine for Nan

Tommy Yurisits ducks, and my fist lands on a taxi's side-view mirror instead of on his head. The real surprise comes later, though, in the Lenox Hill emergency room.

I pressed my forehead against the speaker grill on my grand-mother's kitchen radio. The sensuous voices of the Jaynetts, a one-hit-wonder girl group from the Bronx, vibrated over my face singing "Sally Go Round the Roses."

It was easy to drown out adult conversation by listening to music. My Dad and his mother were in the next room. They spoke low. I barely heard a word, but right after the song ended the disc jockey announced a test for the Emer-gency Broadcast System. A short whistle-signal blew, then the radio went silent and whispering voices drifted in from the next room.

"It's cervical," Dad said.

"Did she get a second opinion?" Nan said.

"Yes. Same results."

"How's Patty holding up?"

Dad started crying. Nan shushed him. I hugged myself tight, imagining Nan wrapping her arms around him. The radio station's emergency test ended. I turned the volume up and listened to Louis Armstrong's "Hello Dolly."

Nan and Dad came into the kitchen two songs later. It was July 1, 1965. I was 11 years old.

"Tommy, Mom is going into the hospital tomorrow and you're going to stay with Nan while she's there, and Rory is going to stay with Nan and Pop Ryan," Dad said.

I nodded OK. I didn't know what "cervical" was, and I didn't want to know.

"How long will she be in the hospital?" I asked.

Nan and me, 1955.

"Not sure. It depends on her recovery speed after surgery," Dad answered.

He said "recovery speed." He didn't pause between the words. I hung onto those two words for comfort, repeating them in my head. "What's wrong with Mom, Dad?"

Dad hesitated. I tried to swallow, but my throat was dry.

"She's having a hysterectomy."

"What's that?"

Dad licked his lips and scratched his nose before answering. "Sometimes a woman's childbirth organs don't work right," he said. "To protect Mom, Dr. Twomby is taking out the parts that aren't working."

In my head, I kept repeating "recovery speed," "recovery speed," trying to build up my courage. Dad waited for more questions. I stared at Nan's cuckoo clock. His face relaxed when I didn't pursue it. We exchanged a grateful nervous look that said, "Let's leave this one alone, and see how it goes."

Mom entered the hospital the next day and I went to Nan's apartment. My grandfather had died the year before, so it was just Nan and me. Over the next two days, when the phone rang, Nan always answered it, even if she was three rooms away. When Dad called, his news was always short.

"Mom's doing OK," Nan told me, but there was no confidence in her voice.

On the third day after the surgery, the phone rang. Nan jumped out of the toilet, barely getting her broad white underwear in place, and answered it.

"Hello," she said, and then yelled "Thank God!" She started crying and handed me the phone.

"Tommy, Mom is doing much better," Dad said. His voice was shaky, but I knew he meant it. I took several big breaths. I felt my heart throbbing. I missed Mom.

"You OK?" Dad asked me.

"Can I see her?"

"Not for a few days. She has gas and is very uncomfortable."

That was good enough for me. Dad was giving me orders again.

I saw Mom at the hospital a week later. I kissed her wet on the nose. She hated that. When she was out of pain, we laughed about the never-heard-before sounds coming out of her body.

"It sounds like Noah's Ark right after the animals had beans for dinner," she said.

I cheered her up, imitating each burp and fart. As we laughed, I felt my heart calming down.

After seeing Mom, Nan and I settled into a routine. A local public school, P.S. 158, ran its daily day camp program from nine to five. Nan worked, I went to camp. She was home by 5:30. I goofed around, stretching my walk home each night so I'd hit the front of her building just as she got out of the car. Nan was the legal secretary for Xavier Riccobono, a senior judge on the Supreme Court (New York's trial court). Every day, the judge or his law clerk would pick her up and drive her home. If Judge Riccobono heard Nan was sick and not coming in, he stayed home for the day. Judge Riccobono was one of the many officials who called Nan "The First Lady of Yorkville."

During the second week of our arrangement, I broke my hand punching a parked taxi's side view mirror. My intended target was Tommy Yurisits' head, but he ducked. I walked over to the emergency room at Lenox Hill Hospital. The nurse asked me whom she should call. I said my father, and then took it back. "No, please call my grandmother."

I figured Dad had enough on his hands with Mom. Plus, the emergency room was a regular meeting place for him and me, and I was in no mood for his "What did I tell you last time?"

Nan was a wild card. She'd never been first on the scene for any of my accidents. It was time to mix it up a bit, and have a different adult yell at me.

A half hour later, Nan swept through the double doors and marched to the corner of the emergency room where I sat on

Nan only has eyes for me, even with RFK on the dais, 1964.

a gurney. I was flipping a bedpan with my good hand. When I saw Nan, I stopped and tensed for the speech.

"How are you?" she said.

A little confused by the opening, I said, "OK, I guess."

The doctor came over to have Nan sign a paper.

"I'm positive his thumb is broken at the base. I'll X-ray the hand, confirm the break, and put him in a cast. He should be OK in five to six weeks," he said.

I started doing the math in my head. I'd be throwing a football by Labor Day.

Breaking into my arithmetic dream, Nan said, "What happened?"

"A guy punched me. I punched back. He moved and I hit a car."

"Next time use your head, it's harder."

That was the entire speech. No, poor baby. No, how many times have I told you, blah, blah, blah. Use your head? My grandmother was talking to me like a football coach. This was a beautiful thing.

Later that night, Dad called.

"Oh, by the way, Tommy broke his hand today. He's fine." Nan said.

I heard Dad yelling in the background. Nan let him go on for a minute, while gesturing to me, shaking her head up and down, and spinning her tongue around the outside of her mouth. Finally, she cut him off.

"Cut the crap. It's no big deal. He's OK and I'm taking care of him."

Dad made a feeble attempt to continue the argument. "Look, you have a short memory. He's a boy. This stuff happens. You fix it and move on. Have a good night and send Patty my love."

Nan's handling of this situation changed our relationship forever.

His Master's Voice

When I deejay on the record player in my bedroom one morning, Dad decides to discuss optimal-volume theory.

Singing along with Paul McCartney on "Good Day Sunshine," I jumped out of bed. The clock radio read 7:30. I pushed up the volume and pounced on my brother in the bottom bunk. When the song ended, I pulled my baby out—the '59 Phillips portable record player in the tweed case with the leather handle. The interior was lined with tan felt and it had a brass speed selector clip shaped like a sundial with 33, 45, and 78 etched into the metal. When I had bought it that yearfrom my friend Joe Skrapits, Dad was not happy.

The record player resembled the suitcase that Jerry Mahoney used when he visited his cousin Knucklehead Smiff. Everything those ventriloquist dummies owned was neat and dummy-sized—little bow ties, little sports coats, and little hats with earflaps. I always worked their show into my schedule.

I figured I had time for three selections before Mom's school chant: "If you don't get a move on, you're going to be late. If you're going to be late, you're on your own. I'm not writing another note to the nun."

I placed the record player on top of my dresser. Being eye level was perfect for tracking the label's logo, song length, and writer—I memorized it all. From under the bed, I retrieved a smaller case with a decal on it that said, "Pepsi, For Those Who Think Young!" I lifted the top to view my treasure, a collection of 45s.

"Pick a winner!" Rory egged me on.

I cupped my hand over an imaginary microphone. "Wake up, sleepyheads, the Professor's here. Our first song is going out to our sixth and eighth grade nuns, Sister Maria and Sister Mercedes. Top of the morning, Sisters! It's time for a Columbia selection, red label, red song." I extracted the record from its sleeve—"Red Rubber Ball" by The Cyrkle—and placed it tenderly over the 45 adapter. My stomach danced when I heard the thump of the needle dropping into the groove. I pressed my ear flat against the speaker.

Out flew music mixed with the worn record's scratches. Rory and I threw our pajamas on the floor and put our dirty underwear on our heads. We hooked arms, swung around, and sang along.

Between the tune's third and fourth verse, Dad joined in. "LOWER THE MUSIC!"

I adjusted it a smidge.

"LOWER."

I opened the door, to let Dad hear the fade.

"How's that?"

"BETTER…AND LEAVE IT THERE."

I shut the door and brought the volume back up. I eyed my next possible selection in its tattered sleeve.

"Scott Muni here, my friends…class is now in session… Let's follow The Cyrkle with a little sweet talk on the Double Shot label from Brenton Wood."

I eased the first selection off and put number two into the spin, "Gimme Little Sign."

Rory and I hummed along while wiggling on our blue school pants.

"DID YOU JUST MAKE IT LOUDER?"

I lowered the sound, went to the door and opened it a crack, leaving only enough room for my lips to get through sideways.

"No, no, no, Dad. It's right where you asked me to leave it."

"I DON'T BELIEVE YOU. LOWER IT MORE."

"OK," I said, while giving him the finger several times behind the door. Rory saluted me.

Dad's beloved RCA Victrola.

With the volume unreasonably low, I dedicated my final selection to Dad. He loved Sinatra. Well, he loved one of the Sinatras. I chose the other one—Nancy snarled her signature "These Boots Are Made for Walkin'."

I circled the room in lockstep. Rory and I exchanged "Sieg heils." On the song's last line, I let it blast.

"WHAT THE HELL?"

"Sorry, Dad. The song was almost over and I turned the knob the wrong way."

Dad's own musical baby, the '55 RCA Victrola, was three feet high and had long gold legs, creamy wood, and a bronze speaker grill. When you opened the top of the Victrola you saw Nipper the dog patiently listening to his master's voice. There was a Victrola polishing rag that lived under the cushion in Dad's chair. Mom wasn't allowed to wash it. This musical temple was off limits to Mom, Rory, and me. We couldn't touch it, but Dad insisted we enjoy its thunder and this infuriated Mom.

In my mind, I see a memory from the music wars with Mom standing over Dad with both hands on her hips.

"Why do you play your music so loud?"

"It helps me highlight the best passages," Dad says and then he points rapidly toward the Victrola. "There, right there, listen to Shaw's clarinet lifting the melody."

"I can't, I'm deaf. You've taken my hearing away."

Mom bangs her hand off her ear a few times and says, "Lower the music, because if you keep it up, I'll pot you."

The Victrola broke once. Dad couldn't fix it. He sat like a lump until our TV repairman, Dominick, made a house call. When Dominick finally got the thing working, Dad's face lit up and his eyes watered. I thought people only wept for joy in the movies, but this scene reminded me of the film *Going My Way*.

At one point Bing Crosby, the young priest, brings the old priest's 100-year-old mother over from Ireland. She shuffles toward her 80-year-old son with her arms out wide, smiling broadly. That would be Dad, giving Dominick a big hug.

Mamma Mia

If a teenager watches a steamy Italian movie on cable, he should remember that his grandmother speaks Italian.

Mom's hospital stay stretched nine weeks. I was Nan Rode's "star boarder" all summer long. Rather than buy wool downtown or shop for three hours along York Avenue, Nan and I did non-Nan things for the first time, ever, like go to the movies. She took me to a James Bond film after a hospital visit. While the opening credits rolled, there was a silhouette of a naked lady with a gun practicing her marksmanship. This pleased me. When Nan noticed the nice lady on the screen, she faked a colossal yawn throwing her arms out wide. She kept her arms at full mast throughout the rest of the credits, completely covering my view, until the good part was over. I'd crane my head up, her arm would follow it. I leaned all the way to the side, and Nan would stretch her arm out like she was trying to hitchhike from behind a large bush. Disappointed, I shrugged. This is what adult women do to little boys. I knew it.

I'd be sitting on the couch watching TV, and Mom would stand in front of me holding up my blanket.

"What the hell are you doing to your blanket?" she'd say.

This humiliated me. We both knew I'd never answer that question. I'd stand there mortified, saying nothing. Then I'd go away, shaking, for a few hours. I dreaded unanswerable questions.

As the summer progressed, Nan and I rearranged our relationship. We were pals and talked more than I ever talked with either of my parents or my other grandparents. Sex was the only area left off the table. After the James Bond incident, I was extremely cautious in Nan's space. The next few years produced no further incidents. I was a master sneak.

By 15, I stayed with Nan four nights a week. My high school was in Manhattan, all my friends were in Manhattan, but my parents had moved to Queens. They didn't like it. I hated their fighting. Staying at Nan's gave me a break from their war.

One Friday night in the early 1970s, I was watching an Italian film on cable TV. It was late and Nan was in bed two rooms away. The film had subtitles and was chock full of sex. Even the music made me horny. I assumed Nan was asleep. I was trying to see if it was possible to jerk off non-stop, straight through the entire film. A tough assignment, but I had faith in myself. Two-thirds in, there was a scene where the actors are making love, and speaking passionately in Italian. This sent me right back to the launching pad under my blanket. Midway through the countdown, I heard giggling and it wasn't the TV. I lowered the sound, and I heard it again.

"Hee, hee, hee."

Oh no, she's awake. Holy shit! She's awake! My pup tent collapsed. My grandmother knew Italian. She was listening to the film. She knew every word. Then a strong rush came over me. She's listening to an extremely sexy film. She knows I'm out here doing whatever, and she doesn't care.

I thought back to the James Bond movie and the blocked view and it didn't figure at first. Then the fog cleared and I got it. When I was 11, I was 11. What was appropriate then no longer made sense. I had expected our relationship to stay frozen. I was slow at picking up on Nan's transitions, allowing me gradual increases in freedom and personal expression. After the movie, in my heart, I bought lace curtains for Nan's room.

Unlike Mom, who could spy me looking at a bra ad through a brick wall, Nan left my stuff alone. I had a few *Playboy, Penthouse, Club,* and *Oui* magazines under my underwear in her apartment. The clothing got moved around, but the arsenal never stirred.

1970, I started seeing my first girlfriend, Ginny. We loved movies and hanging out with Nan. In our first four months

The checkered jacket that goes everywhere.

together, we each gained 15 pounds eating New York Turf cheesecake. Nan knew how to lure company to her roost. For a few months, before agreeing to do it, Ginny and I actually did everything but do it. It was time for protection.

I worked in Corner Pharmacy and had access to a wide variety of condoms. Of course, I couldn't buy them, so I reluctantly stole them. My choice was *Four-Xs*. This item came in a large, blue, egg-shaped plastic capsule filled with lubricant. I thought I'd look sophisticated pulling out one of those. As for an opportunity, Nan was the local Democratic district leader and neighborhood big wheel. The Honorable Ann Pryor Rode spent three nights a week at the Cherokee Clubhouse on 79th Street. Ginny and I picked a night.

We went into Nan's bedroom. Ginny loved the capsule. She felt shy and asked me to turn off the light. Everything worked. When we finished, we spooned for a long time.

"I'm hungry," Ginny said. "Want to eat?"

"Absolutely!"

We made grilled Swiss cheese sandwiches, ate cheesecake, and then I walked Ginny home.

When I got back, Nan was there, sitting in the kitchen and drumming her fingers on the table—no TV, no radio, and no phone. Without a word, she stood up, and nudged me toward her bedroom.

When we got there, rather than turning on the overhead light, she walked to the small built-in reading lamp at the head of her bed. She pulled the metal chain and harsh brightness lit up her pillow. Centered perfectly on the pillow was the condom's plastic shell. Under the unforgiving light, it resembled a suspect under interrogation. Nan motioned me to pick up the capsule. We silently walked back to the kitchen.

Along the way, I held my head in my hands and mumbled, "Unbelievable—first time ever—I'm a shit-for-brains."

She offered me a seat, and then she sat down. She spoke slowly.

"First thing, I like the girl. I'm glad you're using something. Second, don't do it in my bed."

My First Area Rug

Home is where you make it—
and that includes your eighth-grade classroom seat.

I strolled into the empty classroom. Arriving early on the first day of eighth grade, I had my choice of any seat in the house. Of course, this would be subject to the nun's approval. She usually let me stay where I was, provided I wasn't sitting next to a partner in crime. Nuns knew every alliance. They exchanged scouting reports each summer.

My eyes flew around the room. Windows lined one side. The back seat in the window row looked attractive. This position would entitle me to the window-opening assignment for the entire year. The classroom windows were huge and no kid could open them without using the big wooden pole with the metal hook on the end, which stood behind the radiator next to the back seat. The hook fit into the metal hole on the window top and levered the window up or down.

I gave my best trying to entertain Sister Mercedes— I loved her smile.

The pole assignment would get me out of my seat a couple of times a day. Better still, if the nun was facing the blackboard while I was handling it, I could lean over toward the class, and carefully crack someone in the head three aisles away. We called this "knighting the squire." Or, I could lightly tap someone on the shoulder at the same distance, and watch them get aggravated when the person behind them denied doing it. I had to be cautious, though, and reclaim the pole swiftly. Classmates would try to grab it, so they could bring the nun's attention to me. I enjoyed that part the best.

All but decided on my seat selection, I noticed an empty bookcase next to the last desk on the other side of the room. This intrigued me. I liked stuff. I needed a place to put my things. The bookcase beckoned. I went over to the desk, put my schoolbag on the chair, and ran my hand over the surface of the bookcase. Smooth grain, level plane, and each shelf was tongue-and-groove. I loved tongue-and-groove. I didn't like pegged shelving. Dad had shown me the difference when he made a two-shelf coffee table for Mom.

The next day, I brought in my first item for the bookcase, a small vase. I had slipped it into my schoolbag while Mom washed the dishes the previous night. She never would believe me if I told her the reason, so I didn't. At lunch break, I picked a yellow flower from the garden next to the school. I put water in the vase and centered my still life on the bookcase's top shelf. The entire day, Sister Mercedes gave me a single glance with one arched eyebrow—nothing more. This relieved me. I had no clue as to how she was going to react to my squatter action.

But something was missing, and I knew what it was. I needed to accessorize.

The following day, I brought in a lace doily to sit under the vase. It gave my lonely flower texture, comfort, and warmth. I waited for a reaction from Sister Mercedes. This time she was more demonstrative. She reminded me of the bald Scotsman with the bushy moustache in Laurel and Hardy films. Remember how "the boys" tortured him?

Each time they did, he did a double take. He'd rear back on his haunches, hands planted on his waist, and scrunch down one eye while working "the boys" over with his open eye.

When Sister Mercedes entered the classroom she marched down my aisle and stopped at the desk of Attila Krupincza, who sat in front of me. Her eyes bounced over the lace, vase, and flower, and finished off with a long look at me. To minimize eye contact, I pretended to be doing math calculations in my head by looking toward the ceiling and poking my pencil back and forth. I snuck a peek and caught her slowly shaking her head from side to side. I saw her lips move, but the words never made it out of her mouth. This reaction led me to believe that I had limited permission to continue my furnishing foray.

The bookcase had three shelves, all empty and sad. On the third day, I cheered them up. I bought three cheap picture frames at Woolworth's and filled them with magazine photos of my favorite sports figures—Mickey Mantle, Joe Morrison of the football Giants, and Eddie Giacomin of the Rangers. The frames stood evenly apart on the first shelf. Having all three guys there was important, because if one of them got sick or died, the other two still had each other. Sister Mercedes completely ignored the photos.

Over the next few weeks, the shelves filled. I added a dictionary, a thesaurus (I liked words), and a pair of Nan Rode's bookends. Nan Ryan gave me four chipped knickknacks and sour balls in a jar. Dad gave me a clay bust of Rory. It took him a week to sculpt it. I kept my favorite sport magazines, *Street and Smith's Annual Pro Football Issue* and *Peterson's Pro Football Preview*, on the bottom shelf. I had a set of chattering teeth for laughs, and a supply of wax candy for visitors.

One night, I came home and saw that Mom had thrown away our old bath mat. It looked fine to me. It was blue. She saw me pull it out of the garbage.

"What are you going to do with that?" she asked.

"We're doing a school play about the Old West. I plan to use it as an Indian saddle."

Mom rolled her eyes. I washed the mat in the tub, dried it out the bathroom window and brought it to school the next day. It was my first area rug. It fit neatly beneath my feet, edging the aisle on both sides of my desk. With the fluffy rug in place, there was no reason to keep my shoes on. The other kids complained that my feet smelled, but I dealt with those gripes in three ways. I brought in a can of Glade air freshener, I doused my feet with Arm & Hammer foot powder, and I adopted a pair of Dad's old slippers. Mom used Glade as a weapon on all odors, mostly Dad. My grandmother rubbed her feet with foot powder every night after work—she always whimpered and moaned. Dad's slippers? They looked comfy.

To convince Sister Mercedes that my intentions were honorable, I brought in furniture wax and a cotton rag. Every Friday, I took everything off the bookcase and meticulously rode the wood with the rag. I didn't stop until I saw the classroom's overhead lights reflecting off its finish.

Why did Sister Mercedes tolerate this expansion effort? I've thought about that on and off through the years. She was a stern person but had a sweet side. Occasionally, she made fun of herself, made faces, and imitated kids when they were being dopey. There were times I actually loved her.

I think Sister Mercedes was well past her 25th year of teaching at that time, and she may have been getting tired and bored, worn out from teaching the same things over and over, in the same classrooms, to the same kind of students. Many teachers beat conformity into children. They would pummel individuality into dust. Then, when they were done, and the kids were broken, the zombies sat at their desks six hours a day, 210 days a year, in their white shirts, blue pants, and blue skirts. At some point in each nun's career, she must have looked over the sea of sameness and wondered if it made any sense. She is driven temporarily insane and behaves in strange and mysterious ways.

Maybe I was lucky enough to catch Sister Mercedes during such an epiphany. I found my partner in crime wasn't sitting in front of me, or to my side. She was dressed in black, chalk in hand, facing the blackboard.

Schadenfreude

To be a good hater, one must be discriminating.
Case in point: the Dallas Antichrists.

As you get older the word "hate" drifts away from regular conversation. That's a good thing. It's a bad word, and a silly emotion to hang onto. Life's too short.

If you're lucky, you lose it all together. If you're really lucky, you save it all for one person, one thing, or in my case, one professional sports team.

If I hear someone put two particular words together, "Dallas" and "Cowboys," I immediately hate him. If he is wearing a Cowboys jacket, I pray he is overcharged everywhere he goes. If he has a bad haircut, I am thrilled.

For me, schadenfreude heaven is watching the Antichrists from Dallas suffer.

If the Cowboys are doing badly, I stare at the standings the way a GI in a swampy World War II trench stared at his wallet photo of Rita Hayworth in a nightie.

To put it another way: in 1974 the Giants went 2–12. But I wasn't sad. That's because their two rare victories included beating the Texas Antichrists 14–6. (They also beat the Kansas City Chiefs. The Chiefs were coached by Hank Stram, who perfectly fit the response the kid in *Annie Hall* had for Joey Nichols: "What an asshole!")

Here comes Robby Zimmel. He was the most obsessive Dallas fan in Yorkville. How his fan preference came to be still eludes me. How can a New York kid root for a team run by Tom Landry, who was a brilliant assistant coach with the Giants, but who walked away from a potential head coaching opportunity in New York to join an expansion team in a place we stole from Mexico? And how can that same New York kid stand to watch that new team regularly beat the crap out of his hometown Giants?

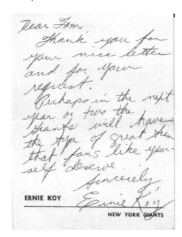

Maybe Zimmel's mother was a rabid Giants fan who, every Sunday during the football season, ignored the kids—no breakfast, no lunch— she watched the game, went nuts, and then, if the Giants lost, she'd give each kid a dollar and tell them to, "Go get something to eat."

That's my best theory so far: Zimmel rooted for Dallas in order to spite his mother!

In any case, there I'd be in Carl Schurz Park in June suffering abuse over how terrible the Yankees were doing, and Zimmel would start busting my chops over how the Giants stank, too. This annoyed me for two reasons: it was June, a full month before football training camp opened, so criticizing the Giants was a sneak attack like Pearl Harbor; second, his razzing would temporarily wipe out my recurring hallucinations that the Giants were getting better.

I was close to putting a garbage can over his head, but I went in a different direction.

As good as the Cowboys were in the late '60s and early '70s, they only won the championship twice. Every other year, they got knocked out of the playoffs.

On the day your team gets knocked out of the playoffs, no matter how well they did during the regular season, you feel horrible. Your world ends. It's hard to eat, music sounds weird, girls aren't as pretty, and it's raining in your heart.

It's the perfect time to reach out to that sad soul.

Moments after the Cowboys lost to the Cleveland Browns in the playoffs in December 1969, I went to St. Stephen's rectory to buy a $5 Mass card.

This was not your cheap $2 card, but the fancy kind—the kind that has a glittering Jesus or Mary in relief on the front of it. (In the Roman Catholic Church, a Mass card is sent to a bereaved person or family indicating that the sender has arranged for a Mass to be said in the deceased's memory.)

There was a prim lady at the rectory desk with bouffant hair and bearing a whiff of Jean Naté perfume. She was very proud of her penmanship and dying to write in the name of the deceased on the card in big swirls. Our conversation went like this:

Lady: "Son, the name of the departed?"

Me: "Can't tell you, Ma'am. Mom didn't spell it for me. She told me, get the card and we'd learn the spelling at the funeral home." I also told her that I would return to give her the name so that the Mass could be said.

Reluctantly, she released the Mass card in exchange for my $5 bill.

I sat on the church steps with the card solid against my thigh and put my calligraphy skill to work, writing out the name of the deceased in beautiful script: Dallas Cowboys.

Adding in block letters: May they rest in peace.

I mailed it to Zimmel, happily spending the extra postage on the fat envelope. My only regret? I wasn't there when Zimmel opened it.

Cowboys to Girls

Playing records on the stoop gets tough when a grownup yanks the extension cord. But that's what lampposts are for.

Ginny put the 45 on the record player and Freddy Muller, Eddie Ekis, and I sang along with the Turtles tune, "Elenore." It was July 1968. Eighth grade was a distant memory that had ended a month before. We hung out on the 83rd Street stoop where Ginny, my future girlfriend, lived. Ginny had fed a series of extension cords out her first floor window, allowing us to plug in my portable record player.

It was midnight. I was supposed to stay over at Freddy's and he was supposed to stay over at my house. But our real intention was to stay out all night until the sun came up and play records on the stoop. Eddie had pulled the same scam. Each of us had our own 45s and we took turns rotating our

Mom loved catching you sitting on a garbage can.

songs into the playlist. We hung onto the words of every tune. Our tastes mingled seamlessly.

Across the street, Mrs. Walsh leaned on her third floor windowsill with a pillow under her chest and arms. I was the unofficial president of the mothers' fan club and out of all the mothers in the neighborhood, we unanimously agreed, Mrs. Walsh was the best looking. Dark hair, yummy kissable face, a mouth like a sailor and oh, that smile. Her uniform was a muumuu housedress that hid her ins and outs. We prayed they'd come out for a peek. Sometimes, you forgot she was up there. I was sitting on a stoop by myself one day, and I heard, "Hey, Pryor, whatsamatter? You look like you lost your last friggin' friend in the world."

Mr. Moylan lived on the second floor of the same building. He resembled the actor Edgar Kennedy and hated us playing "Off the Point" in front of his house. We'd hit the Spaldeen off the edge of the ankle-high ledge on the wall directly across the street. If you struck the ball perfectly off a crack in the ledge, it would zoom off at an extreme angle, gain height, and rocket over the outfielder toward Moylan's build-

"Off the Point" star player, Freddy Muller, winding up.

Mrs. Walsh watching her world go by.

ing. The outfielder would have little opportunity to catch the fast carom off the wall.

That wall had a series of windows, though, and four of them belonged to Moylan. He didn't lean out the window like Mrs. Walsh, but he had excellent hearing. If he was home and we were playing, his windows would fly open and all balls that went in would never come out.

At that point, we had to make a big decision. A Spaldeen was expensive, but this was the best point in the neighborhood. We could move around the corner to a safe ballpark without windows, but the point there was mediocre. We usually stayed put and took our chances. Sometimes, one of us would hit a beauty and we'd all turn and watch the sweet flight of the doomed Spaldeen sailing through Moylan's window.

"Give it back, you bald S.O.B.," Mrs. Walsh would yell, using her two hands to form a megaphone on the sides of her mouth. After the game, we'd go to our locker room—the 403 stoop—plop down, mostly say nothing, and verbally give Moylan the business.

Ginny loved the boys hanging out on her stoop, and Mrs. Chapman, her mother, mostly didn't mind. On warm nights like this one, when it got dark, the music would come out.

Freddy put on the Soul Survivors' "Expressway to Your Heart."

Boom, boom...boom boom, boom, ba-boom
Boom, boom...boom boom, boom, ba-boom

Sometime past one, Mrs. Chapman opened the window and said, "That is your last song." We knew she didn't mean it—Mrs. Chapman was a softy—so when the song ended, I grabbed a new record. But Mrs. Chapman did the unexpected and yanked the wires. The extension cords disappeared back into the window. This was the first time we located Mrs. Chapman's last straw.

I was a mechanical idiot, and Ginny and Freddy looked blank, but Eddie was working on the light pole in front of the building with his house keys, trying to remove the bottom panel. It popped off and Eddie took something out of the base of the pole—a standard electrical outlet with a short extension cord.

"Edward, you're a regular Mr. Science," Freddy said.

"Thank you, Mr. Muller," Eddie smiled, and motioned with his head, signaling me to bring the record player over. I did, and we plugged our music into the pole on the sidewalk, compliments of NYC's Department of Highways— Bureau of Lights, or whatever the agency was called. Eddie and I grabbed a couple of milk boxes and deejayed the tunes, while Freddy and Ginny drummed their sneakers on the stoop.

Around 1:30, we saw Moylan's head pop out of his window and we figured we had ten minutes. That was when the squad car eased to a stop and Officer Bulin joined us.

"What are you doing?"

"Playing records."

"How?"

"There's an outlet on the bottom of the light pole, and we figured it was there for emergencies and things, and this was a thing we needed it for."

"It's too late for music, but I've got to admit, I didn't know there was an outlet in the pole. That's pretty good, but you can't use it because it's only for emergencies, OK?"

"Can we play one last song?" Ginny asked.

"That's it, then, good night. I'm circling the block and three minutes from now, I want silence."

"OK, thank you, Officer."

Eddie put the last 45 on. When the Intruders, "Cowboys to Girls," ended, we put the panel back, closed the record player, and sat on the stoop silently. Officer Bulin came around the block and gave us a soft smile, then he put his head out the driver's side window, cupped a hand by his mouth and yelled up, "Good night, Mrs. Walsh," as she waved down from the third floor.

Born Sassy

*Saucy then and saucy now: Nan tells me
how she razzed my grandfather on first sight.*

Sleeping in the front room of Nan Rode's apartment, I was
dreaming of Ann-Margret in a blue bikini doing a shimmy
dance on a beach whispering my name. "Tommy, oh, Tommy." This vision dissolved when I felt the vacuum cleaner
sucking in my toes, which were hanging over the end of the
bed. Above the roar of the machine I heard my grandmother's voice. "Get up!" She did not like you sleeping when she
was awake.

**Nan, Communion
Day, 1913.**

It was a Saturday morning in the summer of 1972. I looked at the alarm clock on the nightstand.

"It's 8:15!"

"Get up!"

"Why?"

"There's a mouse running around in the kitchen."

I don't believe I heard the end of that sentence while I was still in bed. Mice frightened me. I jumped up, grabbed my eyeglasses, a pair of shorts, and my sneakers, and ran out of the house. From the top of the staircase Nan yelled down to me on the second step where I was tying my sneakers in the low light of the hall.

"Don't come back without a mouser!"

"Huh?"

"A cat, a cat, bring back a cat."

It was particularly hot that Saturday, and the streets of Yorkville were empty. Where was I going to find a cat? I thought about walking up to the ASPCA on 92nd Street but I wanted company for the trip. The only place where there might be someone else up this early was Esquire Deli on 84th Street. Their sodas were ice-cold and Augie, the owner, made terrific hero sandwiches that my friends craved all the time—including for breakfast.

I ran into the store through the open door—the AC was broken—and saw Eddie Hauser talking to Augie's brother, Joey. Augie was at the slicing machine, making breakfast for Eddie.

"Hey, guys!" I said.

I got back three "Yo's!"

I went straight to the soda fridge and pulled out a Mission cream. Walking back to the fellows, I asked, "I need a cat. Anyone want to walk me to the ASPCA?"

Augie said, "Yeah, I'll go. But first go get some ice cream."

"I don't want ice cream."

"Go pick something out."

I'm thinking Augie has lost his mind due to the heat, but I went over to the ice cream case and found the glass top partially open. Looking in, I saw a cardboard box with five snow-white kittens.

"I don't believe it!"

The three of them laughed their asses off. Eddie said, "Take one, take two!"

I never had a cat. This was scary business. One had a pink nose. I grabbed it. The kitten fit into the palm of my hand.

"Thanks!" I said, and ran back to Nan's.

"Jeez, that was quick," she said. It was hard to impress Nan with anything but this almost did. The whole thing took 20 minutes.

Nan was humming to herself as she stroked the ball of fur in her lap.

"Let's call her Stymie," I said. I loved Stymie from the *Little Rascals* TV show.

"OK, but she's a he," Nan said after a quick check under the hood.

The contented expression on Nan's face made me hopeful that I might have a rare opportunity to get inside the lady's head.

"Nan, when was the first time you fell in love?"

With no hesitation, she said, "Your grandfather, Tom."

"Tell it to me."

Nan kept stroking Stymie, who appeared to be sleeping, as she walked to the window and turned on the fan. She came back to the old kitchen table, sat down with the tiny kitten on her broad lap, and started the story. Her distinctive street-wise accent echoed the voices of Yorkville's history:

She was leaning on the railing of the Webster Library stoop at 78th Street across from P.S. 158, with a friend. Tom was late for work, but stopped his brisk walk along York Avenue when he saw the two girls giggling.

"So what are you saying about me?"

The brown-haired girl, whose name was Vera, didn't make a peep. Nan, then called Anna, said, "Oh, we were just saying you appear to be royalty and must be running late for a royal date."

Vera nearly swallowed her tongue.

"Amazing," he said, flipping his cap back on his head. "How did you know?"

"Well, it wasn't that hard. Books are always saying how kings and queens mix with their subjects by disguising themselves and dressing like peasants. One look at the missing buttons on your jacket and the low-hanging socks on your feet...you must be a king."

"Then kiss my ring."

"You don't have one."

Wearing a grin, the young man walked away.

After a breathless pause, Vera recovered.

"Are you nuts?" she said. "You talk to every boy you see, and now you're talking to men?"

"He's not a man," said my grandmother.

"Anna, Hello! He must be 20."

"So what? I can take care of myself."

The girls resumed leaning on the railing.

At this point, Nan coughs a few times and asked me retrieve the wild cherry Smith Brothers cough drops from her bedroom in the front of her railroad apartment. Smith Brothers was my preferred brand, too—I liked the brothers' impressive beards in the picture on the box.

Rolling a cough drop around in her mouth, Nan returned to her story. Soon, the two girls heard a car horn beep across the street, in front of the school. Anna and Vera, recent eighth-grade graduates of P.S. 158, would turn 15 years old later that summer.

"It's him," Vera said. "He has a cigar in his mouth and he's walking over. You are dead."

"Yeah, I can see," Anna said.

"Well, I went to the Tower of London and recovered one of my jeweled rings," the man said.

He presented his right hand. On his ring finger was a cigar band. Anna shrugged, curtsied and kissed the ring. Vera rolled her eyes.

"Can I offer you ladies a lift somewhere?"

"I never travel without introductions. So what's your name?" Anna said.

"Thomas, a king of far lands and horns of plenty."

"Horns on your head."

"Well, I have the royal cab for 45 minutes, so let me take you through Central Park."

Vera spread her arms like an umpire signaling a runner safe at home. Her head bounced like a pigeon's.

"Uh-uh," she said. "Not doing it. Not going anyway."

"Come on, just a little ride," Anna said. "I'm not going without you, and I'm definitely going."

"I hate when you do this. You always get your way and we always end up in trouble."

Grabbing Vera's arm, Anna pulled her across York Avenue and they got in the back seat of the polished car. They went up the avenue, then turned west on 86th Street toward the park.

"So how long you girls know each other?"

"Forget the crap," Anna said. "Who owns the vehicle?"

Vera's mouth fell open, and stayed that way for the rest of the ride.

"I'm not sure," Tom said. "I think it's a doctor from Park Avenue. I just borrow them. The guy who manages my garage works two jobs. He's a walking zombie. He sleeps through most of my shift. Another guy covers for me when I take a car out. I do the same for him when I get back."

"Very nice. I'm in a stolen vehicle," Anna said.

"You like using big words—on your way to Oxford or something? This is a borrowed car. C-A-R. This car will be returned safely without a ding, as soon as I drop the princesses at their castles."

Vera got dropped off first, after several elbow exchanges and whisper battles with Anna.

"Well, Ms. Vera," Tom bowed and said, "It's been an honor serving you."

Vera made a big fake smile and said, "Bye, Anna," while looking at Tom.

Then Tom said to Anna, "Well I don't want you bouncing around in the back and getting injured or anything. There is plenty of room up here with me."

Anna got in the front seat. They drove along.

"How old are you?" he asked.

"Fourteen. How old are you?"

"Twenty."

"Where's your family?"

"After my parents died in 1909, my brother and I were sent to an orphanage. When he turned eighteen, he left and once he was doing well enough to support me he pulled me out of the orphanage. Then I got this garage job."

Tom kept talking and Anna listened for a record long time. He dropped her off on First Avenue and 77th Street—three blocks from her house. Her Italian parents would burn her alive for riding around with a dirty Mick. Tom did not kiss her goodbye although it killed him not to. He always kissed his girls goodbye. This one was different. Pretty, sassy, smart. She had his number and she called him on it. This was something he couldn't live without and she already knew that.

Stymie and Sparky Lyle, Nan's cat and dog, 1972.

Nan stopped talking and stared past me for a few seconds. Then she said, "That's it."

"I want to hear the rest. What happened next?"

"You asked me when I first fell in love, and I answered you. Now get some milk and a saucer for our little Stymie."

Woodstock or Bust

I am set on going to Woodstock despite Dad's opposition.
Then I faint at Grand Central.

"Over my dead body."

This was my father's clear response to my probe:

"Dad, I'm thinking of staying over upstate at Buddy's the weekend of August 15th."

Dad wasn't fully clued in, but he knew enough about the Woodstock event to have set up his personal Berlin Wall against my going. I tried various approaches but was always shot down.

Still, my mind was made up to go and suffer the consequences later. Dad sensed that I was ready to cross a line, and tempted me with tickets to the Albie Booth Memorial Game at the Yale Bowl on August 17th. It would pit my beloved New York Giants against the reigning World Champion New York Jets who were, at that time, an Antichrist equal to the Dallas Cowboys. I was really torn.

It was July 1969, I was 15, only two years out of crew cuts and Dad was still pissed off over that. I was playing tackle football, which pleased him, but nothing about the rest of my life gave him comfort. I was hanging out with every major druggie in the neighborhood. Our crowd was infamous; other neighborhoods sent their druggies to us to clean their neighborhoods up.

Starting in early June, my friends and I would gather at the eight o'clock Sunday Mass at St. Stephen's. No one sat in the pews; we stood in the back. When the priest mumbled the final prayer we dashed out to get the subway to Far Rockaway, where there was no one to interfere with our partying under the boardwalk. There were rundown Victorian houses to play in, and one lone knish stand left on the boardwalk, around Beach 45th Street. Mostly we scattered across the

With Artie Peters on the Lexington Avenue Local, 1969.

sand and had too much fun. I might have continued having too much fun, but, fortunately, I loved playing football. I was younger than most of the kids, as well as a little awkward, but I had lucked into long walks with an athletic redhead named Susan.

A year older than me, Susan lived in Manhattan near Lenox Hill Settlement. She didn't go overboard on the Rockaway fun either; she had followed a burned-out girlfriend into our group. She was going into her junior year at Julia Richman High School and had a wicked book, movie, and song memory. She and I would stroll the boardwalk from 43rd Street to 116th Street and back every Sunday until she didn't show up during the first week in August. Neither did her friend. I didn't have her number or her address and I planned to do something about that, but then I started getting fevers.

On the Monday before Woodstock I was on the subway and was getting off at Grand Central. When I stood up I passed out and fell in the doorway. I came out of it quickly and saw and felt several people stepping over me. A cop helped me to my feet and guided me to a seat. When I was steady, he let me go and I went home. I went directly to a doctor who said my appendix was ripe and had to come out. The next day I was in St. John's on Queens Boulevard. It was my first time in a hospital and I was feeling really down. Whatever I might have decided to do that weekend—Woodstock or the Yale Bowl—I would have missed it. I knew 35 people from our group going upstate and Dad had already bought the football tickets.

While waiting to be prepped for the operation, an orderly came in and said, "A nurse will be in shortly to shave you."

"What?"

"You need to be shaved from your belly button down to the top of your thighs."

"What?"

"It's standard," he said and left the room.

I loved my hair down there. It made you a man. At 15, everyone was aware of who was hairy and who was not, and for the majority of girls and guys, hairy was better than not hairy. I did not want to be bald. I liked being furry and warm. It looked good! A quick review: I was in pain, I could not leave, and now I was going to be sheared! I needed to make something good out of this—and I did.

A nurse was going to touch me. Yes, that was it. A pretty nurse, with a hat and a white dress, was going to address my stuff. In a few moments, my privates were going public for the first time, and I was picturing the lady who would have the pleasure: Barbara Feldon, Agent 99 on *Get Smart*. Now I was sitting up, almost eager to lose my pelt. Anxiously, I watched the door for Florence Nightingale's entrance. I heard noise in the hall. "Here she comes," I said to myself.

In walked a male nurse who looked like Robert Strauss, the actor who played "Animal" in the film *Stalag 17*. This Flintstone-like character with a three-day growth was going to manhandle me. He approached my crotch like a barber, with a razor, a towel and a pan of soapy water. Chit-chat was minimal because all of my focus was on the act. I wanted no slipups so I didn't want to distract him. No names, no nothing. He moved my stuff around like a man does when he shaves, pushing his chin to the side and lifting up his nose. Once he was done, he showered talcum powder on my crotch. Looking down, I saw that my boys were frightened, but I couldn't talk to them until he left. When he did, I tried to calm them down, telling them it would all grow back better than ever.

I had a roommate. He talked only to himself—he said he was moving to New Orleans to fix up his mother's shotgun shack. I was too pissed about my mowed thatch and my lost weekend to care about anything. The Jets beat the Giants 37–14 and I wanted Joe Namath dead.

But I did get a kick out of this fact: Every night, after an orderly came around to give us a juice snack, my roommate got up, put on his clothes and went across the street to the Elmwood Theatre. The movie changed once a week, so he went to the same movie five nights in a row. When he came back he changed back into his hospital gown. I can't remember the name of the film, but this pleased me.

Most of my friends had a miserable time at Woodstock. They stank and a bottle of apple juice was $5. This also pleased me. I spent the rest of 1969 waiting for my garden to flourish again.

Missing the Cool Train

There are many ways to commit social suicide in high school. Playing Mary Hopkins's "Those Were the Days" is especially effective.

September 1968, during my first week as a freshman at La-Salle Academy in the East Village, Brother James Gully taught us English in Room 406. We were reading "A Tale of Two Cities" and it was hot outside. I was sweating at my desk in the window row, which looked out onto the New York City Marble Cemetery, when something started stinking awful. I looked down and there was a pair of gigantic loafers that belonged to the kid sitting in front of me. I didn't know his name yet, but he was a tall black kid with a serious face who was telling everybody who would listen that he was good at basketball. I thought he had a real puss on, plus, his feet smelled horrible. I leaned forward and whispered loudly, "Put your shoes back on."

He shrugged and ignored me.

The cemetery next to LaSalle.

237

I'm second in the blackboard row, with my nemesis, Gumbs, to my left.

"Put 'em on!"

Trying not to get Brother James's attention, I whacked him on the shoulder. Dismissing my suggestion, he turned around and told me to do something rude to myself.

"OK, that's fine!" I said. I reached down and flung both shoes into the cemetery.

That's the day Robert Gumbs and I were formally introduced. We both got punished and he stared at me during detention like a bull studying the matador before his rush. Beginning the next day, he chased after me between classes for two weeks. I was faster then Gumbs. After school he'd wait for me on one side of the building. I'd go into a classroom and look out the window and see which side he was on and run out the other side. By the time he caught me, I had exhausted him. I wasn't in that headlock for more than five minutes.

That was the tone of my freshman experience.

In 1969, during my sophomore year, LaSalle was packed with a student body of 800 boys. The gym served as the lunchroom, and to accommodate all the students, there were several staggered lunch breaks of 30 minutes each. Students sat in the bleachers and most kids brown-bagged it.

There was a lunch tradition at LaSalle—if you left your lunch bag unattended before the meal break, it was passed around the classroom and everyone sat on it, really rubbing it in if they didn't like you. If it worked well you'd hear "Pop!" when a Devil Dog or a Ring Ding package burst open.

I loved Buddy McMahon like a brother, but nothing made me laugh harder than watching him eat two flattened salami on rye sandwiches with runny mustard and watch him push his crushed Yankee Doodles through the broken plastic package the way you work a nearly empty toothpaste tube. Buddy returned the favor many times. It was all part of the school day, and, besides, a flat sandwich had many more bites and lasted longer than a regular sandwich.

Lunchtime was a high-energy point and the teachers knew students needed an outlet. They let us deejay music over the loudspeaker system if we brought in our own records. It was first come, first served. You were supposed to share the dee-

Brother Gully invites Mr. Gumbs to chat about "A Tale of Two Cities."

jay time with other students, but no one did. The turntable was in the gym teacher's office and whoever got there first would lock himself in and play his own tunes for twenty minutes. The top half of the office door was a glass window. This gave your taunters the opportunity to direct threats at you face to face, but likewise, it afforded you the opportunity to taunt them back. Any real punishment of the student deejay would be postponed until he was caught later in the school halls. While he was in the office, he ran the show.

One particular Friday, I brought my 45s to school and I made sure I was the first out of class to dash down to the deejay booth. It was pretty easy to win the race because there weren't too many entrants; most guys were unwilling to bring in their own records. I was a Beatles fanatic and any artist signed by Apple Records was alright by me. I played James Taylor, "Carolina on My Mind," and Mary Hopkins, "Goodbye."

The black and Spanish guys went bananas at my musical choices, banging on the window, holding their fists up and giving me the finger—"That sucks! You're dead!" They wanted to hear James Brown, Aretha, Sly Stone, and Santana. The Italians wanted The Four Seasons—"Pryor, you're a boy ass." The druggies wanted Hendrix and Zappa, but they were cool about it. "Hey, Tee-Pee, why do you play that lame shit? It blows our heads."

Girl-catching eyeglasses with the jacket that won't quit.

I might have played "Get Back" or "Hey Jude," but that would have been too easy. The song I played that sent everyone through the roof was "Those Were the Days" And I don't mean Cream's tune from the *Wheels of Fire* double album. Five minutes before the end of the lunch period, I'd put on the not-cool Mary Hopkins same-named-song and dance side to side, like Soupy Sales doing "The Mouse," and I would wave to the mob at the window, mouthing the words to "Those Were the Days."

It was horribly wonderful.

My decision to repeatedly commit social suicide was never well thought out. It was spontaneous combustion more than anything else.

The Mango King

Rudi, a smooth West Indies stock boy at the supermarket, teaches cute female shoppers the art of selecting the firmest, juiciest mangoes. Whether they're buying them or not.

"Bang!" I heard the glass shatter aisles away. Low to the floor, I deserted my post stocking baked beans. Crawling past a couple arguing over bacon, I slipped through the swinging doors into the meat department. Two other stock boys had beaten me there. We laughed while shushing each other. Sawdust covered our asses. The butchers continued trimming meat, barely acknowledging our presence. Strong collective bargaining and strategic mob influence brought their union a heaven-high wage and insulation from the store's day-to-day business.

Outside the loudspeaker barked, "Bottle break, aisle 4!" Bottle break, aisle 4!" I snuck a peek through the door's small diamond-shaped window. Harry Cohen, manager of Daitch Shopwell Store No. 16, was on the Sky King-style microphone in the store's plywood office high over the register area. On tiptoes, Harry tried to peer over the Plexiglas window blanketed with memos and stock orders. Agitated, he knocked Lola the bookkeeper out of her chair so he could stand on it.

From that high perch, Harry searched the store for a body to draft for clean-up duty. He sought to quell the stomachache building inside him over the upcoming annual store inspection by Daitch's owner, Marty Rosengarten. Near retirement, and hoping for one more bump to his pension, Harry took a swig from the ever-present Pepto-Bismol bottle in his back pocket. Lola used a coat rack to hike herself upright. Finally, Harry spotted his target.

"Menesick, I see you, Menesick. Behind the Oreo display, Aisle 4, Menesick, pronto!"

**Joe Menesick, my fellow
stock boy, 1969.**

I eased back through the butcher's doorway after I saw a
dejected Joe Menesick with his head down, pushing a mop
and pail on wheels toward the accident. I also saw the reason
for the bottle break. Mrs. Curtin and Mrs. Kelly, wheeling
their two carts side by side, were yapping away, oblivious to
their five young boys hazardously circling them and startling
customers. Every Saturday, these two old friends shopped
together with their juvenile delinquents-in-training. The
kids' favorite game? Storewide tag. Harry knew the mon-
sters were good for a minimum of two breaks a visit but
their mothers spent a hundred dollars each on groceries. He
could live with that, but seeing them made all the stock boys
vigilant.

Free to move around again, I went behind the deli counter
to spy on Harry and Lola. After pulling his shirt collar out so
he looked like Mr. Dithers in the comic strip *Blondie*, Harry
realized his stupidity in dumping Lola out of her chair. He
did his best to recover.

"Honey, I'm so sorry."

"Fuck you, Harry," Lola said. Her look at him added
more: "Next time you knock me out of a chair, I'm going

to kick your sad little ass up First Avenue to East Harlem, where I'll finish you off by punting you into a garbage can." Her reaction scared Harry. Lola ran the store. As chief bookkeeper she controlled the finances and wrote the store's reports. Harry's imminent retirement in good standing was tied to Lola doing her job well, and she kept this fact close to her heart—her tiny, stone heart. She was the "Ice Queen."

We knew that Lola preferred girls to boys. Every day she terrorized the cashiers but never bottled up her attraction to the prettier ones. This gave the girls the creeps and the guys loved it. But despite her feelings for the cashiers, it was too much fun bossing a man around, so Lola also kept a man. He was Harold, the store's stock manager. Harold was a black James Bond. If Sam Cooke and Marvin Gaye had a baby, that baby would not be as cool or as handsome as Harold. Tall, smooth, with a soft goatee and a short Afro, Harold wore his store smock like a smoking jacket. Anything on him seemed as if it had been tailored for him—from his T-shirt to his slacks. If I were watching Hugh Hefner's TV show from the Playboy mansion, I would not have been surprised to see Harold sitting between Anthony Newley and Sammy Davis, nursing a snifter of Courvoisier. Harold ran the nonfinancial business of the store. He knew what products moved, and he knew how to milk and flaunt a display.

Soft-spoken, kind, and charming, Harold was the temperamental opposite of Lola. She had no control over Harold's mood and it drove her crazy. But Lola had found the chink in Harold's armor—his blind attraction to her bossiness. Maybe Harold missed a strong woman who had left him early in life, but in any case, Lola shoveled the shit on his plate and he ate it without breathing between bites. This put Harry in double dutch. Lola controlled the books and she controlled Harold. The quality of his pension was tied to them both.

Still crouching behind the deli counter adjacent to the manager's booth, I saw Harry and Lola, but they didn't see me.

"Honey, I didn't mean it," Harry said, rubbing the boil on his neck, twitching his head, and pleading for mercy. "They drive me crazy when they run off and hide like that. This store doesn't clean itself."

Lola fixed Harry with a lingering glare.

"Honey, please don't look at me that way. I feel so bad. Let me make it up to you. How can I make it up to you?"

I didn't want to hear the answer; it would only annoy me. I walked over to the produce aisle. It was noon and I expected the show to start.

Ten feet away, I watched Rudi, our self-appointed "Assistant Produce Manager," lean into and over a cute young lady to show her the art of selecting a ripe mango. This despite the fact that the lady had no intention of buying a mango and that Rudi had no business in the produce section. Phil, our produce manager, had no assistant, wanted no assistant, and kicked Rudi in the ass every time he saw Rudi in his aisle harassing a customer. But at the moment, Phil, who resembled John Cassavetes in both looks and mood, was on his lunch break, allowing Rudi to roam freely.

Phil had his own romantic aspirations. He wanted to date a Miss Subways so he could ride the train, point up to the Miss Subways picture in the advertisement, and tell the guy standing next to him, "I did her."

But back to Rudi. I had witnessed Rudi's West Indies cream chocolate playboy routine several times before, and in any event the Daitch elders would pass on the tale of the mango to generation after generation of stock boys. Most of the store's employees had memorized their favorite details and laughingly reenacted his moves. In fact, only Rudi was capable of delivering his lines with a straight face

That day, Rudi was all focus. He got as close as he could get to the lady's ear without her calling a cop, and said, "Aaah, I can see you a special woman who values this sensuous treat with its sweet, juicy, yellow-orange flesh. Yes? The mango is deliciously rich in fiber and low in calories. It chases irregularity away. Mangoes are a comfort food. They have soothing properties that calm the tummy and bring your belly a full feeling of contentment."

Rudi slowly rubbed his stomach in a circle while moaning low, "Oooooh, ooooooh, oooooh."

A few years later, when Barry White came along, we thought Rudi had changed his name and found a new career. His voice was that deep. When the boys bounced his best phrases back and forth, the conversation sounded like a porno soundtrack.

"It is natural to crave the mango, king of fruits. Selecting a ripe one can be determined by smelling or squeezing the fruit. Here, using your beautiful little turned-up nose, do as I do."

Rudi lowered his head to the fruit and drew in a deep breath like a lover inhales a bouquet of flowers.

"A perfect ripe mango such as this one will have a full, fruity aroma emitting from the stem end. Come, smell the tropics!"

Rudi beckoned the lady to the fruit by sending his bushy arching eyebrows off in long turbulent waves. Rudi found this look dashing. To me it looked demonic. The woman leaned back on her heels, caution bordering on fear lining her face. Her wariness had no impact on Rudi. She reluctantly smelled the fruit in a jerky head move, more spastic twitch than effort to smell.

"Now the final test to ensure its ripeness. A mango is ready to eat when it's slightly soft to the touch and yields to your gentle pressure like a fine peach. Feel how this is so. Feel. Good? Yes?"

Flustered, the baffled woman touched the fruit but then snapped back to avoid Rudi's entwining ivy-like grip. Wetting his lips, impossibly, Rudi moved further in…

"Rudi."

Rudi offered no response to the disembodied voice echoing over his head.

"Rudi!"

A shoulder shrug dismissed a bug.

"Rudi, get a mop. Aisle 2, pronto!"

Rudi's face crinkled all the way up to his bald head. He had unknowingly backed the lady and himself into Harry's sight line. This lone-earring-wearing French-Caribbean Mr. Clean in the sky-blue store smock groaned. As the clock struck twelve-fifteen, the Assistant Produce Manager sadly turned back into a stock boy pumpkin.

The $80 Shoes

*A mirror is Dad's best friend. But even in his pricey shoes,
he can't dance away when Mom has him on the ropes.*

"Don't you like them?" I asked.

Dad sat in his chair, staring at the gift in his lap.

"It's Mickey, Dad. They're Mickey boxer shorts."

Dad raised his head.

"What do you expect me to do with them?"

"You wear 'em, silly, they're silk."

Dad looked down, mystified.

"Mickey Mouse, Dad. Look, he's an intergalactic miner,
with a purple pith helmet, gold shorts, and a silver axe."

I grabbed the boxers, fluffing them out. Dad lifted his head
again. I read his silent message: "Are you out of your mind?"
I looked to my mother for assistance. She ignored me. Either
she was in love with William Powell talking to his dog, Asta,
on the TV, or she was staying out of the courtroom.

Could I have been so wrong? I was positive I'd bought the
perfect Christmas gifts for my parents. In 1969, at 15 years
old, I thought I could paint their dreams.

After all, Mom loved her Seven Dwarfs. I'd bought them
for her knickknack collection. They fit right in with her
Lladros and Hummels. I fixed each plaster dwarf in a special
place inside Dad's handmade shadow boxes, where Mom's
other figurines resided. (Dad loved to make arty items to
please Mom—shadow boxes with two or three shelves for
our walls, a Nativity stable with a fence, miniature furniture
for miniature houses.)

I positioned Bashful on the shoulders of Lladro's "Lady
from Valencia" as her new suitor, and I scrunched Doc,
Sneezy, Happy and Sleepy among the Hummel children
sitting on fences along a country lane. Mom was touched
by my effort, I could tell. She held her hand over her open

A spiffy Dad with his proud mom, Nan, 1946.

mouth, and made a move toward me, then her eye twitched as I shifted her fine porcelain statues around to create my display.

I thought my gift for Dad was also a slam-dunk. He'd been telling me about *Steamboat Willie* and Mickey Mouse's other early cartoons my whole life. (He used my brain to soak up his memories, like a bar rag's sweep at closing time.) Plus, Dad wore boxers all the time. Matched with a Clorox-washed T-shirt, these splendid silk shorts would be half of Dad's warm-weather uniform.

Then my plan's flaw struck me. Dad's vanity trumped his love for nostalgia.

A memory surfaced. Mom, Dad, Rory, seven, and me, nine, sitting in our living room after dinner watching *Mighty Joe Young* on the *Million Dollar Movie* on TV. Same movie, Monday to Friday on WOR, Channel 9. It was our third viewing that week. Mom was reading *Redbook* magazine and Dad, his dress shoes lined up, was polishing them with a power drill. He'd bought a buffer attachment specifically for this use. The drill was loud but Rory and I didn't care; we'd memorized the movie dialogue the night before.

At one point, Mom stepped into the ring.

"How much did you pay for those shoes?"

Dad mumbled a few words, none coherent.

"Come again?" Mom pressed.

"Forty dollars."

"You're a liar. They cost $80. I saw the ad in the paper. They're high-end."

"That's the retail price. I picked them up half-price at a seasonal sale at Johnston & Murphy."

"You're a double liar. I saw the bill. And by the way, this morning someone I know saw you hiding behind a tree on York Avenue, sneak-hailing a cab to work."

Dad faked a cough intended to move Mom along, but it had the opposite effect.

"Well, Mr. Monopoly, how is it you own $80 shoes but my house money hasn't gone up in five years?" Mom asked.

"You're exaggerating."

"You're selfish."

The room filled with cigarette fog. For a fleeting moment, the TV dialogue reemerged, but then disappeared. Mom was on a roll.

"You never owned a shoe with a hole in it," Mom said.

"Not true, my family was broke."

"Little Lord Fauntleroy speaks with forked tongue."

"We had no money," Dad said.

"You had no money because you were wearing it on your head, back, legs and feet. Your outfits could've dressed my entire family."

"My mother worked very hard."

"Worked very hard for her spoiled little baby-waby," Mom sing-songed.

Out of the corner of my eye, I saw Dad's face, though my eyeballs stayed mainly with Mighty Joe. Direct eye contact during my parents' debates involved taking sides. This was to be avoided at all costs. Dad looked like he'd just gulped down a large glass of spoiled milk. Mom had him up against the ropes, working over his kidneys with short rabbit punches, trying to get him to drop his gloves to get in one good shot.

She spoke to Rory and me while continuing to stare straight at Dad. "Hey guys, want to hear a good one?"

I groaned. Rory perked up. Rory was a sucker for indoor fireworks and came out of his pretzel position on the floor, where he had put one leg completely behind his head. Watching him in that pose made my neck hurt. I'd always wanted my own dog, but Rory was as close as I got. While Rory adjusted, I had a conniption trying not to ignore Mom while doing my best to give Dad the impression I wasn't fully interested in what Mom had to say. Mom, five-feet-two with flawless blue eyes, now stood in front of us, arms crossed, and began rocking back and forth in her flowered housedress and lime green slippers. She gave Dad a sappy smile and began.

"When we first started keeping company, Dad took me to see Benny Goodman in the Grill Room. The place was packed."

Mom almost lulled me into thinking this would be a happy parents' fairy tale. I heard sweet clarinet music in my head. But then the music flattened. I remembered why this account had come up in the first place.

Mom swept her raven-black hair off her face. "Right after we sat down, your father excused himself and left for ten minutes. After the show started, he did it again. I looked back to see where he was headed and saw he went through the curtain back up to the lobby. Something was fishy. I followed him. In the lobby, your handsome father was marching back and forth in front of the lobby-length mirror. He was pulling his lapels straight out and tugging his jacket flaps so they were just right. His attention was locked on his reflection, so it was easy for me to sneak right on top of him."

"'Hey, Bob!' I said.

"Dad screamed like a little girl. When he recovered, he said something about needing a little air but I knew. Your father hasn't missed saying hello to a mirror since the day I met him."

I mulled over Dad's problem. His elation over all things old was only tempered by his vanity, and by the fear that people were making fun of him. Dad could hear someone giving him the finger a block away. The possibility that someone might see him wearing Mickey Mouse boxers was enough to numb his feelings for Mickey.

I took the shorts off Dad's lap, folded them carefully, and placed them in his dresser under five identical pairs of size 34 tapered white boxer shorts. There they stayed.

My Chicken Flies

At Ben's Meat O' Mat, I am putting five chickens on a four-bird rotisserie rod. Then one of them flies the coop.

In 1970, desperate to flee my crappy job at the Daitch Shopwell supermarket, I got a different crappy job. Ben's Meat O' Mat was a Mom and Pop butcher shop/grocery store, except there was no Mom or Pop, just two brothers named Pete and Harry. They weren't twins, but they could've been. Wearing porkpie hats on their giant heads, they both resembled Anthony Quinn in *La Strada*. Their massive fingers were boiled frankfurters. The guy smiling on the store's swinging sign was their Dad. He also wore a porkpie hat.

My job was simple: get there early, rotate the stock, deliver groceries, work in the meat freezer. Pete and Harry were poultry pioneers. They told me they were the first butchers in

**Skinny days slaving at
Ben's Meat O' Mat.**

New York City to take the hearts and livers out of chickens and package them for separate sale.

One of my assignments was to dig into the fowl and pull the innards out. Once, while my hand was inside a bird, I thought about the first person to determine that he was going to eat the next thing that came out of a chicken's bottom. What a brave soul. "Here's to the first egg eater," I said to a side of beef hanging in the freezer.

My most important task was spearing the birds. The store's front window was one giant rotisserie with rods full of slowly turning chickens. I loved watching the folks in the street lick their lips as they stared at the rotating, cooking meat. People eyeballed the chickens the same way 15-year-old boys gazed at Jane Fonda coming out of her space suit in *Barbarella*. Store traffic was heavy, which meant I had to be constantly vigilant. When chickens were sold, I was expected to consolidate the remaining birds, take the dirty rods into the freezer, wash them down, and return the rods with new raw chickens ready to spin.

On my first day of work, I walked toward the front of the store with a full rod of four ready-to-rotate birds. As I passed the cash registers, I noticed Pete and Harry shaking their heads in rhythm from side to side. As I placed the skewer into the roaster's grooves, Harry came up behind me and said sternly, "That's not how we do it here."

I made a quick bet with myself that he was going to show me.

"Tut, tut, tut," Harry said. He adjusted his porkpie hat, pulled the rod out of the window rotisserie, and motioned me with his eyes to follow him back to the freezer. Like a baseball pitcher pulled out of the game in the first inning, I followed him down one of the store's two narrow aisles.

In the freezer, Harry took on the role of the weary, seen-it-all veteran.

"Well, Tom, as I told you a few times earlier today, it's five chickens to a spit. Five, always five. This is the reason we do so well. People love our chicken. The birds move!"

"Up yours," ran from my brain to my tongue, but hung there behind my teeth. These were plump Perdue birds. There was no way five of these tubbies could fit comfortably on the standard four-bird rod.

"Tom," Harry continued, "how did we get here?" This was going to be a long lesson.

"How?" I said, after finally realizing he was waiting for me to ask.

"Let me tell you. Dad started a small butter-and-eggs shop fifty years ago, right here at this location. Our Mom was a large German woman and loved her meat. Dad was going broke feeding Mom. He didn't know what to do. His brother Ned suggested he expand the business with beef, pork, and poultry. Selling meat and feeding Mom wholesale saved the family financially.

"A few years later, Dad saw an Italian guy on 86th Street wheeling a barbecue around. When he saw people eating meat off a stick, he smacked himself in the head. He built the rotisserie, the people came, and they never stopped coming. We must put five chickens on the spit. We owe it to our loyal customers!"

While he's yapping, I'm thinking, "You bastard. Your hands are the size of two catchers' mitts. Of course you can slip five chickens on a stick."

He wasn't done.

"So Tom, you sit on a chicken box and place the first three chickens on the spit nice and easy... nice and easy. The first three are a charm. See?"

I nodded my head up and down.

The lecture continued. "Add the fourth chicken and press one hand over it with all your muscle. Now work your free hand over to grip the fifth chicken. While you do this, don't let any pressure off the fourth chicken making love to the third chicken. Then bring the fifth chicken down with equal strength, turning the fourth chicken into Lucky Pierre."

"Lucky Pierre?" I never knew they had a name for the person in the middle of a sex sandwich. Learning this fact was the highlight of my employment.

So, five chickens it would be. I shirked all other responsibilities. My deliveries slowed. Stock sat unrotated. I lifted weights at home. I did push-ups in the store's aisle chanting, "Five to a rod, five to a rod." By the end of the fifth week, tussling chickens onto the spit, going in and out of the freezer, my body broke down. I was losing weight and my stomach was killing me.

I figured staying out of the freezer would slow my death. I dragged a crate of chickens out to the small doorway separating the back of the store from the aisles. There, the chickens and I wrestled without rules. But still, no matter how hard I tried to secure the fifth chicken, it would occasionally pop off. This was not an issue in the freezer. A chicken hitting a side of beef was nothing if no one saw it. But the doorway was in public view.

One day, feverish, fatigued, and soaked through my clothes, I worked a fifth chicken into place. I brought the locknut down. My arm shook. Standing over the rod, I swayed and let out an evil belch. My sweaty hand slipped. The nut flew off, hitting a Cheez Whiz display I was supposed to have dismantled a week before.

The lower chickens pushed with liberated force into the fifth chicken, sending it skyward. It rose up over the aisle, floated for a second, then it fell, slapping the back of a customer's cream-colored coat.

"Thwack."

"Oufff!"

The customer gasped, turned toward me, looked down at the lifeless perp on the floor, and yelled, "Aaahhh! He threw a chicken at me."

I replied, "Lady, do you want to shop safely? Shop at a store where there are four chickens on a spit. Otherwise, wear a helmet."

The following weekend my stomach began to bleed. I spent nine days in Polyclinic Hospital on West 49th Street, calming down my new ulcer. Recovered, I did no further business with Ben's Meat O' Mat and soon returned to my former crappy job at Daitch Shopwell.

Ripple

*It's Friday night and we want wine. So we corner Jojo
outside the liquor store and ask for a little help.*

Here was my formula for a perfect Friday night in May 1970:
One friend and three dollars. One dollar for gas; two dollars
for two bottles of Ripple Red ($1.78) and two bags of Wise
BBQ Potato Chips (20 cents).

Buddy McMahon and I left LaSalle Academy around
three and took the #6 Lexington Avenue Local uptown to
23rd Street. We walked east to the Sanitation Department
pier at the river's edge. Parked way in the back of the long
shed, hidden between two dumpsters, was Buddy's car, a
white '65 Mustang convertible. Buddy slowly backed it up. I
got in. His Dad was a gem letting Buddy drive illegally with

**Buddy McMahon
making his own path
after a fire drill.**

his new learner's permit. It was illegal because there was no licensed driver in the car.

"Pass me the baseball," Buddy said.

I put my hand under my seat and found the hardball and gave it to Buddy. He stuck it in a place that kept the driver's seat from flopping backward and forward. The broken seat, along with the bald tires and several other cosmetic and mechanical issues, made this car an affordable pleasure for a 16-year-old working part time as a Daitch Shopwell delivery boy.

As we drove cautiously up First Avenue, I noticed the five-degree chassis alignment problem that Buddy had mentioned. It felt like we were in a parade and the car was facing the adoring crowd on the sidewalk while we motored straight up the road. It was a pain in the ass to put the rusted top up, so we left it down even though it had begun to drizzle. The busted radio provided no tunes, so at red lights he'd try to idle next to someone playing our kind of music.

On 80th Street, we found a parking spot in front of St. Monica's School. Buddy sprinted up the stoop of his building, and I ran home to my grandmother's on York Avenue. We needed to get into our weekend uniforms—pocket T-shirts (our regular purchase from Arbee's Army & Navy store), dungaree shorts, and Converse sneakers—and I needed to grab my radio.

Twenty minutes later, I met Buddy at 82nd Street and First Avenue. We planted ourselves and waited for someone special. The first guy we asked gave us the finger.

Then Buddy sighted a normally friendly party. "Here comes Jojo."

We quietly cornered Jojo under a candy store awning—like two junkies waiting for the man.

"Hey, Jojo, can you buy us two bottles of Ripple Red?"

Jojo looked at his watch, made a face like we were making him constipated, and said, "OK, but quick. Give me the money."

We snuck a peek at the transaction through the edge of the store window.

The 81st Street staircase at the East River in 2012.

On the way down to the river we bought the potato chips at Eddie's Deli on 80th Street. It was still drizzling. We targeted the spot below the 81st Street staircase on the East River. Under dry cover with our legs dangling over the water, we eased in, relishing our Friday ritual, an al fresco dinner with WNEW-FM on the radio dial.

Mrs. Purtz

"Delivery!" shouts the store manager and I barely beat out another stock boy for the job. I've earned the right to visit Mrs. Purtz, a frazzled, beautiful mother of four whose housedress has faulty buttons.

"Delivery!" shouted Harry, the manager of my Daitch Shopwell store.

I flung the cereal boxes I was stocking into the freezer display behind me, right on top of the Birds Eye peas, and ran to the front of the store. I barely beat out Joe Menesick to the three boxes on the front window shelf. With my victory I won two things. I'd get a dollar for the delivery, and I'd get inside Mrs. Purtz's apartment.

In half of my Daitch Shopwell uniform.

When Mrs. Purtz got up in the morning she looked like a model. That didn't last long. Mrs. Purtz had four sons, ranging from two to seven. Her husband ran some kind of store and was out of the house by 7am to whenever, six days a week. Lacking help with her brood, Mrs. Purtz lost her composure and her hairdo soon after the kids' cartoons.

That Saturday, she came to the store to re-supply. Her boys hung off her shopping wagon like monkeys. Freddy, one of her middle guys, jumped onto an Oreo display and she mindlessly pulled him back. He tried to balance himself by grabbing the top of Mom's housedress. By the time she reached the end of the aisle, three dress buttons were open and stayed that way. Mrs. Purtz rarely adjusted herself. She concentrated on her list as she went up and down the aisles, unaware that she was giving a terrific show. I saw the whole thing from the end of the aisle and moved as needed to continue my surveillance. With a pencil and paper, I could draw for you, from memory, the paisley design that was stitched onto the ample white bra that kept her secret pink parts barely inside the flapping dress.

I didn't care if Mrs. Purtz was a mess. It made her prettier. I daydreamed about her more than about playing halfback for the New York Giants. Mrs. Purtz was better looking than Elizabeth Montgomery, and you didn't have to sit through a crappy *Bewitched* episode—you know the ones without Paul Lynde, Larry Tate, or Doctor Bombay—to enjoy the view.

With her cart nearly full, Mrs. Purtz suddenly turned it around like she forgot something and came down the aisle toward me. As she wheeled by we exchanged hellos. I could smell her salty sweat and her Maxwell House coffee breath when she burped. (Of course I knew her brands!)

Egg boxes were the largest boxes at the supermarket—about the size of a kid's toy chest. We used them to deliver heavy goods. Mrs. Purtz was broke, so her egg boxes would be mostly filled with cheaper items for feeding her mob—cans of soups, french-cut string beans, peas, carrots, wax beans, potatoes, and corn niblets. After fighting off Menesick for the job, I stuffed the three boxes into the giant metal box on the front of the delivery bike. When my brother was small I used to put him in a similar box on a butcher's bike and take a joyride around the block. Rory loved it, but only if I didn't ride the curb, you know, going back and forth from the street to the sidewalk. That turned Rory into a bobble-head doll.

Mrs. Purtz lived down the block from Daitch Shopwell, on East 72nd Street near the building where George Plimpton and *The Paris Review* later took residence. Being healthy and 16, I saw no reason to make more than one trip up the five flights to her apartment. I piled the three boxes on the stoop and lifted them to my chest. Balancing them on my knee, I rang Purtz's bell and entered the hall. The building had a circular stairway so I looked up the center to see if anybody was going up or coming down. When I saw no one, I arranged the boxes directly in front of my face, temporarily blinding myself, and yelled, "Gangway! Gangway!" Then I took off, climbing round and round, leaning my head against one of the boxes and hoping I'd hit nothing until I reached the top.

Mrs. Purtz, familiar with my routine, had the door open as I stumbled into the kitchen and put the tower of goods on her table. Stevie Wonder sang "Signed, Sealed, Delivered," on the radio.

After I was done, I snuck a stare as she went to her purse to tip me. She ran her hand through her thick curly brown hair, trying uselessly to get it back to where it was that morning. Each time she did it, it got wilder and wilder. She looked amazing.

The end of the shopping expedition was, for Mrs. Purtz, the highlight of her chore week. Five boys, counting Dad, were murdering her. Finishing the grocery effort gave her a breather that left her peaceful for a spell.

She kept ice water in her fridge and asked me if I'd like some or if she could make me iced tea. I said iced tea. That took a while to drink, so I could linger longer. I watched her go into her cupboard and get the 4C Iced Tea packets and pour the powder into an old Mott's apple juice bottle, careful not to spill any. Then we talked. Sometimes, she remembered to button her housedress, and sometimes she didn't. I was rooting she'd forget, but it wasn't too big a deal if she didn't—then I could study her chocolate brown eyes.

Demon Dachshund

My girlfriend's dog was bred to hunt badgers and other hole-dwelling animals. There are no hole-dwelling animals on 83rd Street. But there is me.

At age 16, romantic nests were where you made them in Yorkville. There was the Leopard Lounge in Eddie Ekis's basement, so dubbed for the leopard-pattern cover we draped over a stained couch we had snatched from the curb just as the garbagemen arrived. There were the buildings on East End Avenue, where we would sneak in through the service entrances and walk all the way up to the top-floor fire halls. And when the weather allowed, there was Carl Schurz Park.

Teenagers in love shared everything they owned with each other—45 singles, record albums, favorite T-shirts, rabbit-fur lined gloves, knickknacks, and, most importantly each other's entire family. With my girlfriend, Ginny, for instance, came her Ma, Lois; her siblings, Sissy, George, and Norma Jean; and my pal, Ira, the family dachshund.

Before Ginny and I dated, Ira made several attempts to convey his feelings toward me. On cold nights to escape the streets, my friends and I hung out in the Chapman's hallway. They lived on the first floor, and Mrs. Chapman, a widow around 50 years old, was the building janitor. Ira had a short range of emotions: happy, listless, or biting. He saved happy for Mrs. Chapman, listless for most acquaintances and strangers, and he reserved biting for me. Ira bit my foot, my ankle and when he felt especially ambitious, leaped up to nip my calf. Dachshunds were bred to hunt badgers and other hole-dwelling animals. On 83rd Street there were no hole-dwelling animals, and that left Ira terminally pissed off.

When I began seeing Ginny, Ira's attentions intensified. He could smell my fear a block away. Waiting for the Chapman door to open, I'd panic. Seeing the brown and tan blur

A descendant of Ira, Williamsburg, Brooklyn, 2013.

with the crooked little legs coming toward me, stopped my heart. His center of gravity was three inches off the floor and his barrel chest grazed the linoleum. He'd use the kitchen table for cover and zip across the floor to grab my leg. Mrs. Chapman, in her housedress and fluffy slippers, would deliver a loving smile to me as the blood dripped from my ankle into the demon's mouth. In her thick Southern drawl, she'd say, "Oh Tom, Ira sure does like you."

I'd answer, "No, Mrs. Chapman. He likes breaking my skin, and please ask George and Norma Jean to stop cackling and pointing at me."

The Chapman household had its ups as well as its four-legged downs. Mrs. Chapman worked for the public-school lunch program and brought home surplus large-slice white bread, logs of American cheese, gallon-size extra creamy Hellman's mayonnaise, and God's personal gift to my belly, bacon.

Whenever Mrs. Chapman came through the door carrying her tasty supplies, I'd take out a large black frying pan and line it with eight slices of marbled bacon. I remember my disappointment as the black of the bottom of the pan began to reappear as the bacon shrank. I worried that I was not cooking enough. My bacon-cooking style involved wearing a long-sleeve shirt and keeping my head cocked back, to avoid the spitting grease.

Near the end of the browning, I'd get a big plate, four pieces of fresh bread, four thick slices of cheese and, with a tablespoon, plop on the mayo and smooth it to make an even cushion between the bread and the cheese. For good measure, I'd lift the cheese and slip a little extra mayo under each slice. Never using a paper towel to drain the grease, I'd toss the bacon slices directly onto the two sandwiches.

Five minutes after I demolished the meal, the contractions began—rolling tsunamis from the top to the bottom of my gut.

At a given point in the cramp attack, I found the cooling effect of the linoleum floor comforting. I would assume the fetal position, curling myself between the metal of the washing machine and the cool sweat dripping off the pipe trap under the kitchen sink. But it didn't help enough. I begged the Chapmans, "Please kill me!"

The children ignored my pleas. Mrs. Chapman said, "Oh, Tom!" and went back to doing the dishes. Ginny, who liked her men lean, thought it best that I suffer. The only Chapman who gave me comfort at these moments was Ira. As I lay on the floor rubbing my stomach and moaning, Ira would come to me in peace. He'd smell my head and put his wet nose against my face, but he never licked me. This was a truce, not a friendship.

The Growler

Nan's pride is her windowsill flower boxes.
But how she chooses to fertilize them
reveals a different emotion altogether.

"I got hit by a car when I was three." Dad said this so casually I almost missed it.

"What?"

"When I was three. A month before my birthday in front of this house. Right, Mom?"

"Yes—for a change your brother, Tom, was the imbecile," Nan Rode yelled from a room away.

"Car hit me right in the ass," Dad said.

"You're both kidding me, right?" I said.

It was summer 1972. My father, a little under the weather, and I were in Nan's kitchen drenched in sweat after throwing a football around in Carl Schurz Park. We stood at her ancient sink, filling glass after glass under the spout. Her tap water was the coldest we ever tasted.

Then Dad and I sat down at the kitchen table and Nan joined us with her own glass and a bottle of Canada Dry ginger ale. She had a kerchief around her neck to catch the sweat and small curlers that held her hair tight to her head. It looked like someone was yanking her hair and it made me queasy.

Dad said to Nan, "Should I tell it or you?"

"I'll do it," Nan said. She ran her hand across the back of her neck and began: "It all started with your grandfather's growler."

"Huh? I said.

I was surprised because not many stories included the entire family—my grandfather, Thomas Pryor, Nan, Dad, and his brother, my Uncle Tom. Nan resisted talking about her first marriage, the years before John Rode came into her life

Nan and family, 1931, in a rare happy moment.

after my grandfather's death in February 1941. I always felt her sad curtain closing if I asked her anything about him. All I knew was that he had gotten sick. If I pressed her, she would sometimes call him a son of a bitch. I had a feeling that day in her kitchen that some of the blanks were going to be filled in.

As Nan continued, I listened carefully and saw the story she told in my brain:

"Tommy, get the growler," Nan said to her eight-year-old son. In the early 1900s, buckets, called growlers, were filled and refilled with draft beer at the local tavern.

Tommy took the pail from the icebox in the kitchen. His three-year-old brother, Bobby, piped in, "Let me, let me!"

Tommy turned the silver bucket over to his brother, and Nan went to the front window to watch the iceman's horse cart rolling down York Avenue.

It was April 1933, spring's early bloom, and Nan needed fertilizer. There was none better than fresh horse manure. Her plantings were her pride. In the summer you could see the flash of color on her stone ledge from a block away. The four flower boxes stretched across both windows in a military row.

Bobby ran down the stairs and into the street ahead of his brother. Nan leaned out the window and pointed to the target lying on the cobblestones. Not having a scoop, Bobby bent over and took one of his brother's baseball cards out of his back pocket to act as his steam shovel.

Nan directed Bobby.

"Too much, put half back."

Tommy walked over to the German butcher's window to stare at the hanging meats. On the avenue there was only one parked car, the butcher's delivery truck, and a trashcan right in front of it. Distracted by his meat investigation, Tommy missed the deliveryman slowly backing up to avoid hitting the container. The driver didn't see Bobby, and eased his rear bumper into the boy, who fell over face first into the manure pile.

"I told you I got hit at three!" Dad said to me. Nan told him to shut up, poured herself some ginger ale, and resumed her story:

"Thomas, pick your brother up and get up here now!" Nan yelled as the truck pulled away.

Tommy ran over and lifted Bobby up and cleaned him as best he could with a wet newspaper lying in the gutter.

"Wipe it off, wipe it off!" Bobby cried.

When they got upstairs, Nan whacked Tommy "for not watching your brother," then pulled Bobby by his one clean arm over to the washing sink where she took off his clothes and dropped them directly into the cast-iron bathtub. Then she soaked the clothes, put them in the washing basin, ran fresh water in the bath for Bobby, and scrubbed him clean.

Nan then took the growler and walked through the rooms toward the front and the flower boxes. She mixed the manure into the soil with her single gardening tool.

I didn't learn the full story until much later: Although Nan adored her boys, my grandfather Tom was a different story.

Her feelings for him, once confident and strong, had cracked. His bravado and promises shrank down to bullshit. Despite his abundant charm and good looks he never learned how to get along. Tom hated authority and fought with anyone who disagreed with anything he said, and that included his bosses, co-workers, shopkeepers, girlfriends, and bartenders.

He was also a mean drunk who glugged away the little money he made. Poor health and bad habits brought on chronic pneumonia that turned into severe tuberculosis. He ended up at a TB hospital where he spent seven of his last ten years. Nan was tired, tired of being mistreated and tired of working two lousy jobs. She was only 27 and still pretty, but her eyes and spirit were exhausted.

At the time of the growler affair, Tom was driving a cab, a job with no boss that he could anger into firing him. But who knew how long it would be before he got bored or fell ill and went to the sanatorium.

After finishing her chores that day—her only day off in the week—Nan returned to the kitchen, gave the growler a half-assed wash, placed it back on the icebox and began making dinner.

At six o'clock they heard Tom whistling in the hallway. He came in and turned up the volume on the Philco Baby Grand console, the family's one luxury item. The radio cost $50, and it was worth it. In those days, it was the only thing that he and Nan agreed on.

Al Jolson was singing "Sonny Boy," and Tom joined in. He loved the tune and gave its title to his older son as a nickname. Tom kissed Nan on the forehead, his little boy on the lips and nodded toward his older boy and said, "Sonny, get the growler."

Tommy went to the icebox and grabbed the bucket off the top.

"Here's a nickel, go down to the tavern and tell 'em to fill 'er up."

This wasn't a chore. Tommy loved walking into the Old Timers Tavern, where the regulars treated him like a regular and he would grab half a cheese sandwich off the bar. Back in the apartment, he passed the bucket to his father. The growler tipped full with a frosty head of cold beer. Tom poured a glass for himself and took a long pull.

Nan, with her elbow on the worn table and her hand at her chin asked, "How's that beer, Tom?"

"Pretty tasty. Want some?"

"No, it's all yours," Nan said, and the older boy covered his mouth, hiding his smirk.

When Nan finished the story, Dad stood up and walked to the front room. He didn't look happy, probably because I'd heard more than he wanted me to about his father, even if I hadn't learned the whole truth at that time. Dad, like Nan, was close-mouthed on the subject of his dad—nothing but short answers like "He had TB," "He drove a cab," "He spent time in an orphanage."

When I asked Uncle Tom about his father, he said he didn't remember anything about his youth from before he was 16 in 1941—the year my grandfather died. During Nan's telling, I saw Dad ready to interrupt, but he stopped dead when she gave him a stern look.

Nan's expression told me she knew Dad was hung over. I'd seen that drained-of-patience look many times before on her face, and on Mom's. Keenly aware of my parents' intense arguing, Nan wanted Dad to, as she put it, "Cut the crap."

After hearing the growler story I had a lot to think about, but no one to talk about it with.

Back in the Bullpen

I become founder and president of the Sparky Lyle Fan Club, and Sparky finds a way to thank me.

Carlos May wrapped Mel Stottlemyre's pitch around the foul pole. The guy nearest me groaned, threw his program, and gulped his Harry M. Stevens cup of beer. Chicago was up 2–0 in the eighth against the Yankees and my head ached. The night before, I had graduated from LaSalle Academy and I'd celebrated with my classmates by visiting a few York-ville taverns. The next morning there was only one place to heal my pain—Yankee Stadium.

After the homer, many fans left. Four pigeons cooed in-side the copper façade overhanging the ballpark's roof. I as-sumed that they were discussing pulling the pitcher. From the grandstand's last row, I had a splendid view of the sta-dium as I chose my next spot in the rapidly emptying stands.

LaSalle graduation, June 1972.

274

I picked the seat in the right-field boxes that was next to the Yankee bullpen. In 1972, the ushers were harmless and security was lax.

When the inning ended, I zigzagged down endless ramps to field level. Sprinting, I reached my destination soaked with sweat. I lifted my butt off the wooden seat to dry. Hanging onto the metal armrests, I swung myself in the air, smelling the outfield grass. To my right, someone began to laugh.

"I hate when that happens."

I turned toward the voice, and stared into the face of Sparky Lyle, New York's ace reliever.

I lowered myself into the seat. "Me, too," I said.

He stuck out his huge paw. My hand got lost in his as our arms pumped up and down.

"I'm Tommy. It's good to meet you."

"Nice to meet you," the barrel-chested ballplayer said. "You must be a big fan, sticking around when we're playing lousy."

"This is my favorite place on earth."

"How often do you come to the games?"

"Where do I begin? When I was seven, in '61, my Dad's friend passed me from the bleachers into Luis Arroyo's arms in the bullpen, where I met four players. I dragged my father to three straight games in '67 to make sure I was there for Mantle's 500th homer. My Dad and I hugged for ten minutes. I caught him crying. After games, I'd hide in the left field bathrooms so I could sneak into the dugout after the crowd and the security guards left. I got half of the American League's autographs walking with players from the clubhouse to the visiting team bus in the bullpen."

Caught up in telling my stories, I forgot where I was and suddenly it hit me. I'm entertaining the best relief pitcher in baseball.

Sparky was sitting on a bench in the bullpen. We leaned our elbows on the low concrete wall, comfortably sharing the small barrier that separated the players from the fans. Being this close to him was electric. Everything looked sharper.

"Well, you pass the fan test," Sparky said when I finished my stories. He was rocking back and forth with his arms folded against the large NY over his heart.

After the game—yep, the Yankees lost, 2–0—all the players hopped over the bullpen railing. I turned to leave, heard my name and looked back.

"Tommy, it was good talking to you." Sparky's voice was garbled by his wad of chewing tobacco. "You, too, Sparky!" I yelled towards the field.

On the subway, my mind spun as I watched Yankee Stadium disappear behind me. "Nan won't believe this," I said to the blonde over my head, who was lathering Joe Namath's face in a Noxzema shaving cream ad. That year I was living with my grandmother Nan Rode while my parents worked some things out.

I walked through her door. "Nan, we talked for 45 minutes, nearly a whole hour! Sparky didn't move."

Nan was organizing nominating petitions on her kitchen table. As the local Democratic leader, she faithfully shepherded the party's candidates onto the primary ballot each year.

"Nan, I'm telling you, you should've seen it. Sparky Lyle sat next to me and talked to me in front of the entire Yankee Stadium crowd."

"I saw the end of the game. The announcer said the attendance was 9,000. That's not very big."

"Well that's true, but it's not my point. I was talking to the best Yankee pitcher. Me talking, him listening. Then the whole thing the other way. You know, a conversation?"

"Help me count these signatures."

There was no getting through. If she was busy I could tell her that I had just met the Pope in the park and he made me a Cardinal and she'd ignore me.

"Well, Sparky's one great guy and I'm going to make him a T-shirt."

Fortunately, I had some experience in design thanks to my neighborhood wall art. My work at the corner of 83rd and

First Avenue had earned me local bragging rights, in fact. Of course, it had also earned me a slap on the head when my grandmother learned that the cartoon character there, a cross between a horse and a Martian that I called Teddy Ryan, was my signature figure. If she knew this then others also knew it, and the thing she never tolerated was being embarrassed by anyone related to her by blood, marriage, or politics.

I bought T-shirts and returned to the house. Nan made signs and posters for her events, so she had a cigar box full of drawing materials. I grabbed the box and escaped to the front room. I sat on the linoleum floor and stretched a T-shirt out, using heavy bookends on the corners to smooth it down. I outlined my Teddy Ryan, and then I dressed him in a Yankee pinstripe

At the Cornelia Street Café, 2009.

uniform. His two antennae stuck out through the baseball cap. I sketched the stretch socks perfectly. He was waving one hand and leaning on a bat with the other. I used a Flair pen to emphasize the pinstripes on the uniform. I lettered "Sparky Lyle's Fan Club" in Old English font. After yelling at me for using her club supplies, Nan said, "Nice job. What are you going to do with it?"

"I'm giving it to Sparky."

"You're full of crap. Get back in the kitchen and help me count. I've got three candidates who need miracles."

It was a good shirt. I made myself one, too. If Sparky was going to have a fan club, it needed to be bona fide. I was the first member and president of the club. I also made shirts for four friends—Buddy, Eddie, Benny and Smithy.

That Friday, the five of us returned to the Bronx wearing our shirts, with Sparky's folded neatly inside a brown bag to keep it clean. This time, it was difficult to get near the bull-pen. A rent-a-cop saw my shirt and gave me a thumbs-up. Sparky was becoming a fan favorite and rent-a-cops were fans, too. I slipped Sparky's shirt out of the bag and held it up so the cop could see it, and then I made a pleading head motion toward the bullpen. With a brief look, the cop gave me limited privileges to run over there.

Sparky was on the bleacher side of the bullpen talking to one of the ushers. I yelled and held up his shirt. He busted out in a grin and came over.

"Here you go, Sparky. I made this for you."

I turned and pointed to my friends a section away. They pulled their shirts down and stuck out their chests.

"Congratulations, Sparky. We're your new fan club."

Sparky held the shirt up against his jersey and showed the other players in the bullpen. A few laughed and applauded. A few rolled their eyes.

"Are you coming to the game tomorrow?" Sparky asked.

"Absolutely!"

"Good. I'll wear it for good luck."

I felt bliss.

When I got home, there were four old ladies sitting around the kitchen table. Petitions were everywhere. I knew two of the ladies, but the other two were strangers. They were eating my food, drinking my ginger ale, and ruining my amazing news.

"Nan, I gave Sparky Lyle the shirt."

She ignored me, "Pauline, give me the count again for the 500 block on 83rd Street."

"Forty nine, not including two dupes," Pauline said.

I said, "Hello…the ballplayer accepted my shirt."

Nan to Annie: "How many do you have for York between 81st and 82nd?"

"I'm all fudged up, let me count 'em again," Annie answered.

"Well get unfudged and stop screwing around," Nan decreed. "We'll do this right and be done tonight."

I tried one more time.

"Nan, I'm not going to work on tomorrow."

I had her attention.

"You're not going to work?"

"I'm going to the Yankee game."

"You're not going to the game. You're working."

I blabbered on, about the shirt, Sparky Lyle, and that he was wearing the shirt for good luck and that I had to be there. We compromised. I'd work until noon and then have someone cover for me.

The next day, we, the five fan club members, caught the end of Yankees' batting practice. I hoped to see Sparky before the game but couldn't find him. Dejected, I spent the first six innings locked in a funk. After many assaults, I got near the bullpen but there was no Sparky. I asked the other players, "Where's Sparky?"

"He joined the army."

"We traded him."

"Who are you, his wife?"

I didn't know the Yankees had so many comedians. I didn't know if Sparky was in the ballpark. The Yankees were up 3–2 going into the eighth, but the first two batters got on base. The Yankee manager came out of the dugout and raised his left arm. The crowd roared, and I knew it before I saw it. Sparky hopped over the bullpen fence.

My heart was on the outside of my chest.

Sparky intentionally walked the first Texas Ranger batter he faced, Frank Howard, loading the bases with no outs. The next batter struck out swinging. Cheers! The following batter struck out looking. Two out. Bedlam!

By this time, I had lost my friends and my sense of place. I knelt in the aisle behind the Yankee dugout. Sparky readied to pitch. I prayed.

He threw a nasty slider. Strike one!

Second pitch. Fastball. The umpire's right hand went up. Strike two!

Sparky looked in, reared back, and let go. Foul, back to the press box.

I couldn't take it. He rubbed the ball, returned to his stance and delivered the pitch.

A crackling slider. Strike three!

The crowd erupted. Sparky strutted toward the dugout banging his glove to his chest. I rose from my knees and screamed, "Spar-ky, Spar-ky, Spar-ky!"

As he crossed the foul line he spotted me, pointed, and then began unbuttoning his jersey. After the third button, I saw it.

Sparky was wearing my shirt!!! I saw my calligraphy, I saw my horse head. I saw my pinstripes bleeding ink straight down the middle of his chest. Sparky winked at me, and then disappeared into the Yankee dugout.

When I got home, Nan was alone doing the wash.

"I saw your T-shirt on Channel 11."

"You watched?"

"Yeah, we finished the petitions early. WPIX did a close-up when Sparky opened his jersey. What happened to the ink? It looked like he was bleeding."

"The ink ran. I used a Flair for the pinstripes."

"Why didn't you use a ballpoint?"

I shot the breeze with Sparky many times that year. He let us throw a few around in the bullpen. He was warm. He was funny. He was a regular guy.

In 1972 you could sit next to a ballplayer at Yankee Stadium.

Sources and Credits

The WPA Guide to New York City, Federal Writers' Project, 1939, reprinted in 1992 by The New Press.

"Anchors Aweigh" (1906) by Charles A. Zimmerman & Alfred Hart Miles.

"Drink, Drink, Drink," aka "The Drinking Song," from "The Student Prince" (1924) by Sigmund Romberg & Dorothy Donnelly.

"Meet Me Tonight in Dreamland" (1909) by Beth Slater Whitson & Leo Friedman.

"Pack Up Your Troubles in Your Old Kit-Bag" (1915) by George Henry Powell & Felix Powell.

The following chapters were first published in substantially similar form in the following publications:

"The Headlock That Won for the Giants," copyright © 2008 by The New York Times Co. Reprinted with permission.

"The Third Beer," copyright © 2008 by The New York Times Co. Originally published as "The Boy in the Bullpen." Reprinted with permission.

"My First Area Rug," copyright © 2012 by The New York Times Co. Originally published as "One Foot Planted Firmly in the Nest." Reprinted with permission.

"Indoor Tackle" and "Dad's Promise," copyright © 2012 by The New York Times Co. Originally published under the combined title "When the Fire Hydrant Was the End Zone." Reprinted with permission.

"The Family Car," copyright © 2012 by The New York Times Co. Originally published as "Cooling Off in Bethesda Fountain." Reprinted with permission.

"Spotless Cleaners" and "Davy Jones' Locker" first appeared in A Prairie Home Companion online. "Davy Jones' Locker" originally published under the title "My First Coffin."

"Rory," "The Holy Cart," "Ladies in Black" (originally published as "Developing a Habit"), "The Girl Who Killed Santa," "Over the River and Through the Potatoes" (originally published under the combined title "Thanksgiving 1961"), "Herman the German" (originally published as "A Barber's Portrait of Kaiser Wilhelm"), and "Schadenfreude" (originally published as "Schadenfreude—How 'Bout Those Boys?") all appeared first in Mr. Beller's Neighborhood online.

"My Chicken Flies" appeared first in Underground Voices Magazine online as "Poultry in Motion."

"The Growler" appeared first in Opium Magazine online.

"Mamma Mia" and "A Valentine for Nan" appeared first in Ducts Magazine online under the combined title "A Valentine for Nan."

All photographs are by the Pryor and Cuccia families with the following exceptions:

Photographs on pages 213, 221, 222, 223, and 243 courtesy of Jan "Sissy" Chapman.

Photographs on pages 171, 198, 211, 234, 237, 238, 239, 240, 241, and 258 courtesy of Patrick Cullinan.

Photograph on page 154 courtesy of Marty Dougherty.

Photograph on page 189 courtesy of Gerard Murphy.